CAMBRIDGE LIBRARY COLLECTION

Books of enduring scholarly value

History

The books reissued in this series include accounts of historical events and movements by eye-witnesses and contemporaries, as well as landmark studies that assembled significant source materials or developed new historiographical methods. The series includes work in social, political and military history on a wide range of periods and regions, giving modern scholars ready access to influential publications of the past.

Life in the Niger, or, The Journal of an African Trader

First published in 1862, William Cole's journal records his experiences in the highly challenging circumstances of a trading expedition to Africa. Cole outlines in graphic detail the dangers he had to endure, and describes how he 'surmounted the most glaring difficulties'. Often displaying a wry humour, Cole's memoir speaks directly to the reader, with a tone of immediacy. In an anecdotal style, he describes the customs and costumes of the natives, and their often hostile reactions to him, and recounts how he was regularly without food, arms or assistance. The journal tells of the barbarity and cruelty he witnessed, alongside occasional acts of kindness or amusing situations. Cole's thoughts frequently revert to England, displaying his homesickness and his longing to return. Describing his life in Africa as 'a mixture of smiles and tears', Cole paints a vivid picture of a European in Africa during the mid-nineteenth century.

Cambridge University Press has long been a pioneer in the reissuing of out-of-print titles from its own backlist, producing digital reprints of books that are still sought after by scholars and students but could not be reprinted economically using traditional technology. The Cambridge Library Collection extends this activity to a wider range of books which are still of importance to researchers and professionals, either for the source material they contain, or as landmarks in the history of their academic discipline.

Drawing from the world-renowned collections in the Cambridge University Library, and guided by the advice of experts in each subject area, Cambridge University Press is using state-of-the-art scanning machines in its own Printing House to capture the content of each book selected for inclusion. The files are processed to give a consistently clear, crisp image, and the books finished to the high quality standard for which the Press is recognised around the world. The latest print-on-demand technology ensures that the books will remain available indefinitely, and that orders for single or multiple copies can quickly be supplied.

The Cambridge Library Collection will bring back to life books of enduring scholarly value (including out-of-copyright works originally issued by other publishers) across a wide range of disciplines in the humanities and social sciences and in science and technology.

Life in the Niger, or, The Journal of an African Trader

William Cole

CAMBRIDGE UNIVERSITY PRESS

Cambridge, New York, Melbourne, Madrid, Cape Town,
Singapore, São Paolo, Delhi, Tokyo, Mexico City

Published in the United States of America by Cambridge University Press, New York

www.cambridge.org
Information on this title: www.cambridge.org/9781108031226

This edition first published 1862
This digitally printed version 2011

ISBN 978-1-108-03122-6 Paperback

LIFE IN THE NIGER

OR, THE

Journal of an African Trader

LIFE IN THE NIGER

OR, THE

Journal of an African Trader

BY

WILLIAM COLE,
(OF LIVERPOOL.)

LONDON:
SAUNDERS, OTLEY, AND CO.,
66, BROOK STREET, HANOVER SQUARE.
1862.

LONDON:
SAVILL AND EDWARDS, PRINTERS,
CHANDOS-STREET.

LIFE IN THE NIGER.

"Tales of fiction and of life,
Tales of bloodshed and of strife,
Tales of villany and wrong,
Tales of paganism strong;
By solving such we learn the arts,
The civil and the savage parts
Of man's creation."

AUTHOR'S SCRAPBOOK.

It is now some years since I paid my first visit to the sun-scorched shores of Africa, and that visit was to Lagos, at one time the most noted slave depôt on the western shore; but, as we have all heard by this time, it has been captured by the English, and a few years hence may be a most improving and a profitable colony.

My present outset was under the auspices of the late much-lamented Macgregor

Laird, who was, in truth, a most indefatigable pioneer.

A voyage to the coast has so often been the theme of my contemporaries, that to sit down and write that of my own would be a digression at once tedious to myself and to my readers; therefore we will presume that we have before us, not the fair land of Poland, but that of oil and negroes.

We are at the entrance of the Niger, and our vessel is rolling to and fro upon the troubled breast of that most pestilential river, the Broes. Our arrival has been observed, and the exploring steamer, *Rainbow*, comes forth to meet us. It is night, yet not a moment is procrastinated, for we are anxious to greet our companions, and they to receive intelligence from home. A general fraternization ensues, and the morn breaks in upon us, and then a loud huzza is raised, and we enter the Nun entrance of the Niger. The scenery before us is not very striking.

At the expiration of five days (during which period our vessels were attacked by the natives, and Captain Wild, in command of the *Sunbeam*, was shot) we arrived at Abo or Ibo; here I am to stay and conduct the trading operations of the expedition. From this date I shall commence my Journal, August 12th, 1859.

The first greeting I received upon my landing, was a peremptory order to go to hell. Turning round, anxious to learn who it was that would be so obliging, I encountered a smiling piece of animated ebony, shaking his fist in a very impertinent manner in my face; certainly not a very calm reception, thought I, but on I passed, and soon learnt from my interpreter, that such as I had received, was in accordance with the established rules of Ibo welcoming. Five days hence, I again take up my pen to record a native naval engement.

Before my factory runs the ever tepid river, and right before my chamber-window the following events took place. For two days previously I had heard, from private sources, that a skirmish was to take place, and that the brothers, Tschukerma, Ajie, and Akia (but more of them anon), were to assemble and meet together, with their united forces, upon the beach, and there to display their tactics for the edification of a revolutionary prince, one Bama Pier, who lives within the precincts of Abo the less.

Towards five o'clock this present Sabbath morning, I was suddenly aroused, not by the cheering sounds of chanticleer, but by the yellings of the excited Abohnites, who, all eager for glory and renown, had rushed to the play-grounds (excuse the term). In a few moments I was up and at my door ; upon this, a shout was raised by the mob, a party of whom came forth and saluted me. A shaking of hands ensued (of which I retain a feeling remembrance), and I left them outside to discuss the probable results of the contest.

As my watch proclaimed the hour of nine, another shout was raised to welcome the arrival of his highness Prince Akia, who appeared in his state canoe, propelled by fifty athletic paddlers. On this occasion a homœopathic dose of grog was, by the prince's command, bestowed upon each and every one of his followers. Towards the tenth hour, old Tschukerma appeared before the factory, at the head of some sixty Amazons, all ready for the coming conflict. Upon every head was carried a huge bundle of bludgeons; in either hand they bore the sinews of Nizerian warfare, in the shape of pikes, javelins, assaigais, and muskets. Tschukerma then formed his company into a presentable position, and there left them standing at ease, whilst he betook himself to my factory. Here he most cordially greeted me, and sate himself down to await the coming of Ajie, who came at eleven o'clock. Although not booted and spurred, he looked eager to give vent to his almost proverbial bloodthirsty propensities. His retinue consisted of a judicious coupling of Amazons and gladiators, each and every one of them bearing a disjointed member of defunct mortality in their left hand; javelins and matchets were carried in their right. Presently he entered my house, accompanied by Akia. Here they seated themselves, and began discussing matters, whilst ever and anon their opinions were washed down with mia oebo, or rum. Leaving our heroes to enjoy themselves, we will view their costumes.

Akia, the opulent, was robed in sky-blue velvet. His breastplate of leather was studded with cowries and other symbols of paganism. Upon his occiput he wore a low-crowned broad-brimmed hat, with a golden band and buckle. Of course he wore the white hawk's feather. In his hand he carried a small baton of lignum vitæ, covered over with tinsel and cowries.

Tschukerma, the eldest, and their chief, wore a petticoat of fancy cloth. Round his waist was girt a band of leather, profusely ornamented with cowries. Upon one of his shoulders was affixed an epaulette. His well-formed head was covered with a worsted cap of divers colours, in which was inserted the white hawk's feather, and worked over with many little trinkets of paganism. In his right hand he majestically wielded a large parti-patterned umbrella.

Ajie, the brutal (his looks told me so), wore his usual war petticoat of red baize, covered over with cowries and brass buttons. Over his shoulders was thrown, though not ungracefully, a native tibric, or cloth. Upon his head was reared a huge hat, colour red, in which was inserted two white hawk's feathers. Whether this hat was made of beaver, sheep or goat's-skin, deponent knoweth not ; but this I will say, that I have never seen its fellow. Well, let me add, that around this hat were fastened some twenty brass mirror cases, and I can assure you it formed a very conspicuous helmet. I have since offered to purchase this hat, but as he wants the devil and all for it, I leave it in his hands. In his hand he carried a small ruler (which he had stolen from me upon his introduction), and with which he would playfully tap the "nuts" of his adherents. To complete his make-up, his eyes were tastefully set off with a chalk outline.

For three hours these mighty potentates sat together enjoying their

"Otium cum dignitate,"

whilst the opposing party was almost out of patience. At length it was proposed that the meeting be postponed until the morrow, as each and every one felt more inclined for food than warfare. My advice was asked, but *Hudibras* furnished the reply—

"For those that fly, may fight again,
Which he can never do that's slain;
Hence timely running's no mean part
Of conduct in the martial art."

And so thought they, for the next movement was a move off.

The morning came, and so did the

heroes. They met, they yelled, and danced most satisfactorily until dinner-time, when a palaver was commenced, which resulted in the total upset of the whole affair, for no further hostility was to be feared on either side. The performance over, the troops retired, each individual as full of dignity and consequence as the "Iron Duke" himself. This is no bad idea of Nigerian warfare; for when a meeting of a rival community takes place for the purpose of trying the force of arms, the matter is generally prolonged to such a period, that all thought of an immediate action ceases, unless a hereditary curse is the cause, when the children of the disputants will hereafter meet, and fight in honour of the dead.

I have mentioned the wearing of the white hawk's feather. I may as well tell you that such is proverbial; but no man is allowed to wear, or even possess one, who has not killed his man, or a leopard, both of which are considered of equal value. It matters not how you may have killed your victim, so that you have a skull to produce when called upon to do so.

A few days subsequently, a fellow came to me for an emetic.

"Is it for yourself?" was my question.

"No, sir, for my master."

"Who is your master?"

"Tschukerma."

Not having seen the individual before, I resolved not to grant his request until I had made myself acquainted with the truthfulness of his mission. Dismissing him with the intelligence that I would shortly be in the town, and would call upon Tschukerma, towards sunset I rode over to the palace of the prince, where I found him alone, and wrapped in his sovereign

(20s.) cloak of meditation. He seemed very surprised to see me, nor did he seem to treat me with the same affability as he was wont to do; but he invited me to sit down, which I did, and saluted him.

"Ah, ah! Oĕbŏ," he replied, "I sent my slave to you for medicine, and you refused to give it me."

I plainly told him that I was not accustomed to "dash" medicine until I knew for what cause it was required. This seemed to satisfy the old gentleman, for he told me that his wife had been making gŏmhor, and that she had very unfeminine thoughts in her head, to dispel which the gods had counselled her to apply to me for an emetic, for the purpose of making her disgorge whatever food she might have eaten that day. I managed to stifle a laugh, and, again mounting, I rode homewards, having promised to fulfil his request.

As a connecting link to the chain of events that will in due course follow, I have added a few notes of a desultory character.

THE SIGNING OF PEACE AFTER WAR.

If there has been a war of any lengthened duration, it is generally settled in the following manner:—

The two head-men engaged in the disturbance, purchase conjointly an Albino, that is, a creature born of coloured parents, but possessing a most remarkable pinky complexion, and easily obtained at a marketable price from its progenitors or holders. An Albino is anything but a pleasant personage to meet with, especially to the European; their eyes are pink, and their wool is of the lightest; their skin seems unhealthy, and is rarely, if ever, free from ulceration; in fact, their close approach greets your olfactories rather too keenly to be relishable. Such is an Albino, and he is brought forward and set between the head-men aforesaid, who, placing one hand upon his shoulders, seize his hands in theirs, and drag him forward, declaiming aloud that war is over, and should either of them (the chiefs) have cause to fight again, it must be as allies, or not at all; should this vow be broken, the family of the offender is to be seized upon, and liable to be sold into slavery. Upon this, they swear by the Albino's blood; an attendant quickly advances, and strikes off the head of the victim, whilst the chiefs uphold the body.

Taking a walk the other evening, accompanied by the eccentric Mousa, my attention was drawn somewhat suddenly to the said individual, who respectfully asked me "whether I saw de moon."

"No," was my reply (for as chance

would have it, a passing cloud had partly obscured the heavenly beacon); "what for?"

"Cos, sar, you can't tell im what dem moon am gone in de cloud for."

"No," replied I, somewhat interested.

"Well, sar, you see it be var cold up der, and de moon, he go behind de cloud to keep his self warm. Ah, ah, massa, cunning coon dat moon, massa."

A few days afterwards, the same individual displayed great tact and ingenuity in the execution of the following.

Sitting down to my breakfast, I had occasion to remark that the sugar was rather dirty.

"Deed, sar, he be clean nex time."

Leaving the table, I chanced to peep into the pantry, but judge my surprise when I absolutely saw Master Mousa in the amusing act of washing a huge lump of sugar in a basin of water.

His surprise was equal to my own when, to his chagrin, it was observable that the sugar was dissolving.

"Ah, massa," said he, "he run away, and me no see im."

This was enough for me, and so I left him.

The secret (if it be one) of palm oil making, and its subsequent disposal, has perhaps never before been rendered to the public; but if it has, there can be no objection to my giving a detail of the process in my own words.

The palm-nuts grow in clusters or bunches, containing as many as four thousand, and when gathered, are thrown indiscriminately into a trench or pit; they are then covered over with leaves, and so left until they become somewhat decayed; the manufacturer then jumps upon the nuts, and by so doing presses out the oil; the refuse is then parted, and the oil is placed in pots containing from twenty to three gallons. The kernels of the nuts also contain oil of the most transparent nature, but so tedious is the popular mode of extraction that it is but seldom obtainable, otherwise than boiled, and then its colour is very dark, and the taste unsavoury.

Palm oil is also used as food, and the mode of making it is very superior to that of making the traders' oil. The nuts procured as before stated are pounded in a mortar, and when sufficiently bruised are then thrown into a pot containing water; this is then allowed to boil, and the oil rising to the surface is skimmed off gently and allowed to cool, and, I must say, a nicer relish is seldom required to render the bachelor's yam palatable.

When the oil is brought for sale, it is in pots, as mentioned before, and when we do buy it, it is generally after a great deal of anxiety and talk. When a trader calls upon you, he also brings with him all the followers he can raise to his standard, and by so doing completely fills your palaver room with stenches of the vilest description. The majority of my readers are perhaps totally unaware of the odour arising from a congregation of unwashed negroes; but when they bring us oil, we are anxious for its purchase, therefore it is that we are not particular as to their cleanliness.

Trade is not prosecuted in this vicinity as it is in England. No, no, my tyro in the art of bartering, you will find the motto here to be, "every man for himself, and God for us all." The first advance made is to observe the frontispiece of your customer. Do not treat him with contempt, though his cloth be of the coarsest, for he may possess a puncheon or two of oil, and yet he brings you but a couple of pots, which are, in very many instances, a shrewd test of your trading capabilities. Treat such a fellow with caution, blind his forwardness with a glass of grog, a Kolă nut, and a little soft soap; lather him well, and you may expect a respectable per centage in the shape of produce, which is all we want. If you cannot at once strike a bargain, do not lose your temper, but take the matter quietly, and suit yourself to circumstances. In opening your trading operations, you need not be in any hurry to name your own price, but calmly ascertain what is wanted by the seller, and when such is known, you do not excite his covetousness above a certain degree, and you have a chance of beating about the bush until you are enabled to secure the prize at a marketable valuation. I would have you also to bear in mind, that small profits and quick returns pay the best; and also, in every instance, let your own penetration and sagacity be at work, or you may be the loser; for the negro has a wit of his own, and has discretion enough to use it.

One afternoon I was leisurely smoking my pipe, when a thought of home so bothered me, that I took up a piece of chalk and manufactured the following upon the head of a puncheon:—

"Oh, Mary, sister dearest,
Your face is pale and wan,
And all your mirthful joys
Have vanished one by one.
The cottage now is lonely,
The days are long and drear,
For, Mary, we do miss thee,
My sister Mary, dear.
My sister Mary, dear.

Oh, Mary, sister dearest,
I prithee be more gay:
The cheerful birds are singing
Unto the flowers of May.
Then why not look more happy,
Though thy face betokens pain;
In sadness we do miss thee,
Then prithee smile again.

Oh, Mary, sister dearest,
How happy is thy smile;
I would not it should be
For others to beguile.
I know that thou art happy,
I know that thou art here;
Without thy smile we miss thee,
My sister Mary, dear.
My sister Mary, dear.

Of course the generous reader will pardon this humble effort of the African Trader, who has in simple language attempted to depict his veneration of one whom nature bids him cherish.

On the 10th of November, 1859, the *Rainbow*, under the command of Captain Walker, left here, conveying Lieutenant J. H. Glover and the Rev. Samuel Crowther, a coloured missionary, from Lagos, both of whom were connected with this expedition, and now returning to the mother country in search of repose after their tedious exertions. I am now alone, not a white man is there near me, nor have I the means of communication with any, for I am one hundred and twenty miles from the sea, and in a country the aborigines of which are much to be dreaded, and never to be trusted. I have no interpreter, so I suppose I must learn their vernacular by compulsion; but as Captain Walker purposes returning to me with men, money, and material, at the end of three weeks, I may as well suit myself to circumstances. Another feature to mark the day herewith presents itself, I mean—

THE DEATH OF KING AZAKA

The spirit of this venerable man took flight early this morning; he had long been laid aside by the native empirics as an object incurable. His son has already laid claim to his deceased sire's property, although the defunct cannot be cold as yet.

The dead Azăkă was a pleasing instance of self-promotion. He, to a certainty, was of noble birth, that is to say, his father had been an influential chief, but his progenitors were poor, and he (Azăkă) had to fight his way; poverty reigned predominant, and the non-fulfilment of a speculation made him a slave, and he was sold. When he began his bright career, he had but a thousand cowries in the world; but so well did he lay his plans, that in a year or two he was in possession of a good canoe and a couple of slaves. With such assistance he, in time, migrated to a tract of uninhabited land; here he felled the trees, and reared a threshold for himself and followers. A short time afterwards he was followed by a troop of runaway slaves, who sought his protection, and finally acknowledged him as their king. At this time, Obie was the king of Aboh, but being an improvident fellow, his extravagances compelled him to seek relief from Azăkă. It was granted, and a subsequent period finds him in possession of the major portion of the town of Aboh, where for many years he has lived and reigned in peace; and now that he has gone to his fathers, the event is about to be celebrated by a human (or rather inhuman) sacrifice. The pleasant duty of headsman is bestowed upon the son and heir, who will, to his own shame and satisfaction, behead and otherwise torture some forty individuals. The *modus operandi* is as follows:—

Each doomed wretch is bound, and goaded on to dance, and while the assembly are loud in their praises of the dance, a number of torches are held on high to gleam in the midnight, and the butcher advances and with swoop after swoop severs the heads of his victims. This over, the burial of the dead demands attention.

Towards nightfall, several females sought my domicile and claimed protection, saying they had fled to save their lives, as Horsyne, Azăkă's son, was murderously savage, and was slaying everybody in his excitement.

A day or two following, Prince Tschukerma paid me a visit. One of his lady attendants seeing a fork upon my table seized upon it, and began to comb her wool with it.

John Locke, the high admiral of the river, called upon me, and was so delighted with a concertina, that he broke it open to see where the music came from.

The young king of Oko also paid me a visit; but as he is of little consequence at present, we will say no more about him.

Being greatly in want of provisions, I thought it would be better for me to go over to Irdoni, a small town some four miles off, and purchase them. I started about nine o'clock, and, after a long pull, we arrived at the market-place. Here, much to my surprise, I was immediately surrounded by the eager, gazing Irdonites; in fact, I was forced to land, and, by so doing, I was necessarily escorted by some two thousand natives, many of whom had never seen a white man before. A score or two would approach me cautiously, and set off again at full speed. Several ladies—though very ancient ones—made bold to stroke my hair, and snap their fingers in token of surprise; my hands were subjected to a close examination, and so were my eyes; but the sum total of their observations prompted them to assert that I was not of woman born.

Many an aborigine of the far interior was to be seen; in fact, every town of note had its representative in man or material. Several of the females excited my fancy amazingly, not on account of their beauty, but the unsightly length and breadth of their hair. One of them had a knob raised perpendicular to the astonishing height of four feet. How she managed to make it stand erect became to me a matter of concern and observation, but a close inspection soon enlightened me. These were my observations: upon the top of the head was placed a cap of wicker-work, into which was inserted a slender stick or cane of the desired length; over this the hair was trained to twine itself, and then plaited; this done, the plaits were cemented together with a mixture of cane-wood and palm-oil.

The market-place exhibited a curious display. Here would be found an ancient dame loudly proclaiming the merits of her plantains, soap, and fue-fue balls; there would I see a pretty, long-necked damsel, a perfect beauty to look upon, with a well-washed calabash, deeply laden with Guinea grain and corn. Passing onwards, a country showman would exclaim—"Please to hobserve the negro merchants a-eating of their food out of a chamber hutensil."

Orlsăquă (*Anglicè*, God willing), the king, came forth to greet me. Agreeably to his invitation, I repaired in his company to the palace, where his Majesty treated me with every kindness and consideration. For some time we sat together and conversed, my seat during the time being a leopard-skin. I was forced to move about. His Majesty having noticed how uncomfortable I was, called for one of his stoutest slaves, and, making him lie down, expressed a desire that I would make a seat thereof. I declined the honour, and proceeded to arrange for my departure, but he would not let me go until I had consented to sell him my waistcoat—which I did, to save any unpleasantness—for a goat and two fowls. During the latter part of our interview, he proposed that I should wed one of his daughters, but the honour was respectfully declined; nevertheless he still maintains that I am his Ozgono, or son-in-law.

We parted after mutually shaking hands. This Orisăquă was formerly a slave, but, like Azăkă, he has fought his way; is of stately build and proportions, and may be forty years of age; he is a good trader, and worthy of especial recommendation to any person about emigrating to his vicinity.

Wending through the market-place on my way to the boat, I was again subjected to a counter-scrutinization. My mission over, I embarked with my purchases of dried fish, a couple of goats, and about one hundred eggs. An hour afterwards I was at home. where I found a messenger from my friend Tschukerma, with the pleasing intelligence that the natives of Orŭ, a tribe who are opposed to my trading here, have sunk carronades of the largest trade calibre to impede the progress of any ship ascending the river. As a word of advice to all after-comers, I would have it distinctly understood that the surmises or rumours circulated by any Nigerian tribe, if of a hostile temperament, should not be discredited, but ample means should be used to sift any such information thoroughly. Nor would I have you place too much "confidence in princes," for a little friendship is a dangerous thing, especially in such a region as this; for friendship is often used as a cloak by which the assassin seeks your destruction. However, I accepted the information with thanks, for at this time the river is very shallow, and any attempt to ascend would result in the loss of craft, and a fearful death to all hands. I have been drawn into this digression merely to render my narrative as serviceable as possible to those for whom it was written.

On the following morning the king of

Oko called upon me. His visit was of the briefest. He seems to be an intelligent fellow, but his ingenuity was severely tried, judging by the many conjectures he uttered concerning the utility of a skylight. He could not find a use for it, but, anxious for information, he sought the aid and wisdom of his sagacious pedagogue, Hoōderĕ, to solve the mystery. The schoolmaster was abroad, and inebriated, so I had to volunteer an explanation. I next permitted him to view his person in the speculum, but I could not get rid of him until I had "dashed" him a silk handkerchief.

Towards sundown I took a stroll along the beach, where I encountered several youthful sportsmen amusing themselves by wading up to their knees in water, and with pointed darts, shot from rudely-made bows, pierce the bodies of the fish as they came within view.

Wending onwards, the following incident brought me and my peregrinations to a stand-still:—

To render my scene imaginable to the reader, I must be permitted to picture some fifty large canoes, and every one displaying a huge lamp. Aboard of them are seated a numerous assemblage of negroes, some clothed with parti-coloured pantaloons, part of a coat, a battered hat, or, as the case may be, a remnant of the attire worn by civilization. A goodly number of these individuals are in a beastly state of intoxication. What with the effluvia (anything but odoriferous) arising from liquor, their skins, and clothing, to say nothing of oil and tobacco, it is enough to upset even the stomach of an African trader, to whom, through necessity, such aromas form the air he breathes.

One of these slave merchants (for such were the drunkards) had lately purchased a woman and her infant; she was in irons, and put aside to await her transportation. Presently, the same dealer bought a male serf, who was also handcuffed and set aside. The poor fellow, with a tearful eye, took his allotted seat, but a moment had not elapsed ere he had discovered in the face of the negress and her child the stern reality of his lost wife and offspring. In an instant they were locked in fond embrace, and the babe once more enjoyed the fond caressings of his sire. In the happiness of the moment, all troubles and perils past were forgotten, the tear was allowed to run its unchecked course, and a smile of hope lightened up their faces. Alas! how soon do we find a cherished notion fall? So it was with them; their new possessor had watched their emotions and smiled upon their grievings; these he allowed to subside before entering and displaying his African brutality, by felling the husband and consigning him to the depôt for another trader, who returned a suitable exchange.

For the readers of the many narratives concerning Nigerian exploration, the loss of European life has perhaps formed the most memorable trait; it is now my intention to give one instance of gross indignity shown by these barbarians (the Ibos) to the white man's body.

About two o'clock, in company with my predecessor, I took a walk as far as the resting-place of the late Dr. J. G. Batchelor, who, it must be borne in mind, departed this life after a severe attack of dysentery about two months ago. The grave is situated about a mile from the factory. Upon our arrival thereat, we were thrown into the utmost excitement by the apparent desecration of the grave; the corpse had been removed, but for what purpose, our feelings for some time allowed us not to conjecture. After a little hesitation, we came to the conclusion that the natives had stolen the body for the purpose of fetish making, for which, beyond doubt, the white man's body would be highly esteemed. A sad fate, forsooth, awaits us all, but such as this we little dream of.

The head-man of the Itabues, or Brass traders, called upon me, and most bitterly complained about trade. One fellow told me that he had lost twenty slaves last night. (Well I knew it, for I had sheltered two.) The traders are greatly incensed at our continued residence here, and to-day they gave vent in various ways to their displeasure; however, to soothe their animosity, I gave their chief a "dash" amounting to a guinea. This done, I was asked for permission to kill some rats inhabiting one of my outhouses. The wish gratified, the whole fraternity set to work and caught some sixty good-sized ones; these I was assured would form a glorious feast.

Ajie, the usurper of Aboh (but more of him anon), is on the beach holding trading palavers, and I believe he has gotten the precedence over the Brass traders. Of one canoe which he visited, he made an offer for the entire cargo, which not meeting the owner's views, was politely declined; and the upshot was, Ajie ordered the trader to leave Aboh before sundown, under pain of confiscation of self and cargo. Considering the disposition of Ajie, I thought the fellow got off very easily.

I may as well add that I was robbed last night; but, as I have before said, Ajie is on the beach. I have some reason for asserting that I am his prey.

On the succeeding morning, Prince Akia arrived here from the up-country, bringing with him a goodly number of slaves and a vast amount of oil, all of which the Brass traders are eager to possess. It is a thousand pities that we are without those essentials, grog and salt, as I make no doubt trade might be done both expeditiously and profitably. The courteous reader will be assured that it was a pleasing sight to see the arrival of his canoes, each displaying some fifty ensigns of barbaric device, the paddlers pulling to a tune or rather song of two notes, a natural.

Towards evening we had a very smart shower, but it did not mar the pleasant aspect of the beach, the margin of the river being lined with canoes, each outdoing the other in the brilliancy of their lights. Were it not for the villany afloat, one might fancy himself on the Cheshire side of the Mersey. The aborigines of Aboh and of Brass are nightly to be seen putting their bodies into the most excited postures, and displaying their terpsichorean propensities in their curious dances; the air is filled with the most inharmonious sounds, elicited by a man and two sticks from a huge log of hollow timber called a drum, by which they time their "rounds so joyful." Many of the gentler breed are seated around an immense fire, thus picturing to the fancy a a certain Fire-office tenanted by the elite of Pandemonium.

This day brings forth another month, a month so much enjoyed at home, and with it comes the stern reality of Christmas. One cannot help thinking of the great preparations now filling the heads and the hands of the good dames of Britain; really the contrast is striking. Here am I, in the midst of nature unadorned, uncultivated by civilized hands. At home (i.e. in England), the fond maters are beaming with gladness anxiously anticipating the coming 25th, when every now absent member is supposed to meet, and to garnish the festive board with his or her presence; loud are the sweet congratulations, and proudly does the son and heir give honour to his sire's hospitality by declaring—

> "It was my father's custom,
> And so it shall be mine."

Loud will be the peals of merry, merry laughter, when round the yule log the youngsters sit, each their future fate foretelling; and yet the mistletoe bough and holly bush must be swept away, and the happy crowd dispersed to battle through the world. But I have digressed too far—now to business.

Arose this morning by first cock-crow, and when I sallied out, my ears were greeted with shouts of the most ardent and enthusiastic description. The cause,

I learned, was, that Akia had just succeeded in selling some thirty niggers.

Although this is the holy day of rest, and well known unto the natives, it is no more respected than we have a right to expect; therefore we enter the house in no pleasant humour. Just before I commenced my customary duty of reading prayers to my people, I sent a message to Akia, requesting him to suppress his playful manifestations for an hour; or, if not, to lessen their noise as much as possible. But of course my request could not be granted; peradventure they fancy religion was never made to render pleasure less. Therefore I had the pleasure of aping Spurgeon with a diminished head. Any individual cultivating or capable of appreciating the excellence of foreign melody, by all means should make a sojourn here, and if he be not satisfied, after two or three practical recitals, with native talent, I will simply consume a palm-oil chop.

As Aboh, the present seat of myself and avocations, will a few years hence become a vast depôt for miscellaneous trading, I will endeavour to make the reader acquainted somewhat with the town, and with the aboriginal rulers thereof.

Aboh is in the hands of the usurper Ajie. Here let me describe him. He is of some six feet ten inches high, and about fourteen stone in weight. He is as black as we in imagination consider Satan. In disposition he is as fair a realization of his demoniacal majesty as one would wish to find. His past actions and his present bloodthirsty propensities stamp him at once as the Nana of his country. His eyes are large and habitually dilated. His head is of the bullet species, and covered with a surface of crisp, short, woolly hair. His physiognomy is the acme, in the phrenological sense, of well-stamped villany and cunning.

Next in significance comes Akia, a tall, stout, blustering fellow, of some thirty-three or thirty-five years of age. He has the swaggering gait of an over-fed Dutchman. This, no doubt, is caused by a tremendous rupture, from which, at intervals, he most acutely suffers, as may be expected. He is as big a scoundrel as his brother Ajie, but, commercially speaking, he is more adapted for the slave Rialto than for the seat or station of a barbarian prince or tyrant; he is rich, and therefore dreaded by the people. As a trader he is energetic and enterprising. As a specimen, let me add that I have bought as many as twenty puncheons of oil in the course of an hour from him. In rotation comes Hootie, the most despicable of this brotherly trio. He is of immense bulk and proportions; in fact,

Daniel Lambert would fail in comparison. Be it said he is not over-industrious, and necessarily insignificant; therefore let us leave him in peace to enjoy his plenitude of fat.

Tschukerma comes next, though I ought to have placed him first. He is the chief of all the chieftains (but Ajie, bear in mind, usurps his authority). He has seen full half-a-century or more, and still possesses the vivacity of youthful manhood. He is of comely build and exterior; his features are eminently benevolent and kind, and his qualities are excellent; but his disposition is so mild and unassuming, that he has wasted one half, and consents to waste the remainder of his existence in retirement amongst his children, wives, and niggers. He is, without exception, the most faithful coloured friend I have ever met with; in fact, as will hereafter be related, were it not for him, my life would be in diurnal jeopardy. As a statesman, in all public matters he claims precedence, always excepted the period of his inebriation, when, as a matter of course, he stays at home and cultivates a further intimacy with his pagan theocracy.

This digression, however, brings us to the subject to which I intend to devote some consideration for the benefit of any unfortunate after-comer.

Bottle of Beer, a young Krooman in my employ, at the request of Tom Liverpool, the chief of the Kroo gang, went on the beach to meet a very acute Brass trader who had cheated Mr. Liverpool to a small amount. The fraud having been discovered, the defrauded wished for the restoration of his money Bottle of Beer, bent upon his mission, was observed by Ajie (who is on the beach selling slaves), and by his orders he was put in irons. This having been reported to me, I went over to Ajie, and demanded by what right he had caught one of my men.

"Did you not," was his reply, "capture two of my men, and keep them for three weeks, and then make me pay a bullock (the universal compensation for wrongs) for their release?"

"Quite true," said I; "your men were caught in the act of stealing, and I can assure you they got off very easily."

"Well," said he, "I have your man, and will keep him. As to the property found upon him—ha! ha! why I will sell it."

Upon hearing this, the numerous bystanders set up a loud ha! ha! in appreciation of what was said by Ajie.

By this time I felt my dander riled, and replied, somewhat haughtily—

"Well, Ajie, I am a white man, and for this insult you shall atone."*

"Ah!" said he, in reply, "white men have died here before." (Hereupon he enumerated his fingers, and looked up musingly, exhibiting three). "Yes," he added, "three of your brothers have been killed, and your queen spoke of revenge, but she does not think of that. All that she requires (here he mimics the voice of one of our company) is plenty of 'ile.'"

Calling to memory the fate of Car and Lander, who were murdered in this vicinity, I calmly replied—

"Remove your salt, or liberate my man."

"No," said he, "I'll sell him; but touch my salt, and you shall die."

"This, then, is gratitude. You would

* Two or three days ago I had lent Ajie six puncheons to stow salt in. This salt is still in my yard, and under the vigilance of my people.

murder the white man for protecting the black?"

"Yes," said he, arising and calling loudly upon his jue-jues for strength to carry his threat into execution should I touch the salt.

Until now I had been passive; but my British birth had been insulted, and I would have felled him. I made a menacing gesture, and Ajie was conquered for the moment; he turned lazily round, and sank upon his mat. Silence now prevailed, and we parted, but my man was still a captive. I now set to work to defend my premises, for I anticipated a visit from his satanic highness.

Towards noon Bottle of Beer returned, having been released by Ajie's orders upon the condition of receiving four pieces of cloth, when it could be procured "unknown to me," in addition to what had already been forfeited.

Thus you see, gentle reader, who are no doubt a philanthropist, although the flag of Britannia is floating over my domicile, it is outraged. What an idea for a man to come out here and to trade, and by so doing civilize this degraded people, or, if preferred, to be starved by degrees, and then hurried onwards with a dose or two of cruelty! Most grossly and most cruelly have I been insulted by this fellow, but how can I repulse his indignities? Picture my position. I am the only white at this place, my men are two, a coloured assistant and a cooper (the Kroomen are leaving for the Confluence); with these two individuals I have to prosecute my trade, manage the factory, and furnish brains upon every exciting occasion. I am now beginning to learn the pleasures of my position. I have not a weapon (save half a poker), and as to food or ammunition, I believe I may procure the former at Fernando Po, and the latter at Powell's, South Castle-street, Liverpool, with equal facility. Should the natives feel so disposed, they could easily murder us, and under our present burden our fates would be signed, sealed, and settled, the property confiscated, and our dwelling burnt. The people have a peculiar notion that, should a white man be killed, a puncheon or two of oil will gladly be accepted as a full compensation. The idea has probably arisen from the following incident:—

One of the carpenters engaged in the erection of the factory, visiting the town, called upon Ajie, who offered him a seat. During their conversation—I know not what the subject was—the parties grew warm and excited. Ajie then spat in the carpenter's face; in a moment the insult was returned, a scuffle ensued, and Ajie received a thrashing, but in rushed an overpowering number of niggers, who fell upon, stripped, and finally pummelled the carpenter. Ajie upon this was pleased to order the carpenter to be completely denuded of his apparel, and exposed to public gaze and ridicule. The mandate was strictly enforced and obeyed, and there he lay in a most pitiful condition for two days and nights, during which period he had not tasted a morsel of food, but was told to feast upon his own excrement; in fact, some was actually forced into his mouth. During the third day, rumours of the ship's approach were in circulation, and the carpenter was set free. When the ship did arrive, the matter was laid before the captain, who possessed ample means for enforcing redress, but the matter was completely arranged upon the receipt of a bullock. To this day

Ajie brags of what he did on that memorable occasion.

The carpenter-hero of this narrative, it must be understood, was not a white man, but he was a free man, and possessed the same rights and privileges. Surely, patriots whose hearts have bled, and will bleed for freedom, right, and peace, will be alive to future revelations from this vicinity. The desecration of the dead and the destruction of the living European, ought to act as an incentive to all future comers to arm themselves with a stock of strength and decision, and a full determination to struggle manfully with pagan insolence.

December 7th.—A great number of the Brass traders left here this morning, taking with them plenty of slaves. I may ask whether they manage to get rid of their living freight for doubloons or not in the neighbourhood of Acassă Creek, it being a famous corner for private trading.

It may be interesting to know that the charge for transporting yourself and commodities to the Confluence, a distance of some one hundred miles, is no less than 15*l*. Of course you will have to furnish your party with an ample supply of provisions.

Provisions at this season of the year being so scarce, and we so ill provided, we are necessitated to divide a fowl, and so make it serve us for three days; however, we managed to eke out a subsistence with fried yam and pickles.

25th.—The anniversary of all that's sumptuous, but to me it is a day never to be forgotten. Even the tone of the temperature is cold and unpropitious, but my people were clamorous for a feast, therefore one was arranged. Towards eight o'clock my colours were hoisted, and twenty men, including my own and some few stragglers, sat down to a repast consisting of three fowls made into broth, to which was added a small portion of rice, and fu-fu, or mashed yams. Palm-wine was also in abundance. Towards evening my guests treated me to a dance by the "light ob de moon," with a kettle-drum accompaniment.

Four days subsequently brought the scoundrel Ajie to my factory, his object being to rob me, and to dispose of some oil, all of which I bought, after a deal of unnecessary palaver. In fact, my being so defenceless has subjected me completely to his caprices. I do not consider my property safe, and I may say as much for my life. Twice has he threatened to slay me to-day. A javelin in one instance was thrown at me, but fortunately with little effect, for I picked it up, and intend to keep it as a memento. Everything Ajie sees he wants, and, if not given him, he will possess it either by force or stealth. He knows how weak my position is, and he takes advantage of it; but I have sent for Tschukerma, who is, and ever has been, my friend and supporter.

On the following morning, my friend came, and I laid my case before him, but he shook his head, and plainly told me that he would endeavour to shield me from harm, but as to the property he would not guarantee its safety. This is the last day in '59, and yet I feel as though I had been struggling in this vicinity for years instead of months; it is midnight, and yet I am forced to be about, poor devil that I am. Is there no consolation in store for me? Hark! I hear a timid tread; it is—it is the footstep of the nocturnal thief: bang goes my revolver—by Heaven, he falls! A groan is heard, and I, to complete the year, have a companion in misery, by name Obunzobi, and a right-hand man of his most Satanic Majesty, Ajie, King of Aboh.

> " Life is a game we are bound to play;
> The wise enjoy it, fools grow sick of it.
> The losers we find have the stakes to pay,
> That winners may laugh, for that's the trick of it."

1860.—This day beginning the new year, I was highly pleased to find that several of my traders had brought me some oil, but as I make it a duty to suppress Sunday trading, I declined the purchase until to-morrow.

The morrow came, and so did the oil, most of which I purchased; and having a little grog on hand, I "dashed" it to my traders, who thus became very comfortable, and promised to extend their transactions. In the evening I had a slight attack of fever and ague, but after a good sweating between the blankets, I arose next morning quite recovered.

Three days later, Tschukerma again paid me a visit, and I invited him to breakfast; we then began a palaver, the substance of which, my readers will not be surprised to learn, was Ajie's gross and most brutal conduct towards myself; and his advice to me was, "Remove the factory" (for which an immense sum had been paid) "to the opposite side of the river, and keep a sufficient number of hands to protect your property" (I have before said that I have but two), "for you may depend upon it that as long as you live in such an unprotected state, you will never be free from Ajie's molestations. You know him, and without assistance there is no help for you; for we cannot take up arms against our brother, but if possible I will protect you. My own son, you must know, is hidden in the bush, for Ajie would poison him if he had a chance." Tschukerma then sent for his son, who came, but was immediately sent away again, the old man looking after him until the distance proclaimed him gone.

Before leaving, I presented the good old fellow with a jacket, a silk handkerchief, and half-a-dozen mirrors, as an earnest of what he might expect if he persevered in his good offices.

As a specimen of what a trifling opportunity for petty theft will produce in the shape of a commotion, I have inserted the following.

After Tschukerma had left me yesterday, I felt pretty certain that I should be free from insult, at least until I heard from him again; but judge my feelings when I heard that my steward, Mousă, was hotly engaged in a palaver with a decrepit old hypocrite named Ojecodie, who, it seems, had by some means or other gained possession of Mousă's gun, and that gun being my property, I was early upon the field of dispute, and demanded an explanation.

It seems, whilst Tschukerma was engaged with me yesterday, he had sent Mousă (who is a slave of his) to bring the son and heir of the Aboh king to visit us. Upon his return, he laid his gun down, whilst he betook himself to the beach to wash: when preparing to come home, the gun was not to be found. After a good search he was told that it was in the possession of Ojecodie, who refused to give it up, or explain how or from whom he had obtained it; but there it was, and for its restoration he demanded five thousand cowries. This I deemed preposterous and insolent, and again demanded the gun; but a few of Ajie's serfs assembling, and hearing my request, surrounded and laughed at me. Not liking such an exhibition, I very politely floored one of the foremost; and a spirit of determination, added to a few more stout raps, brought quietness back again, and the old hypocrite sued for pardon, which was granted. From what I have since heard, I am led to believe that the gun was stolen merely to test my temperament.

This is the Harmattan season, and from its effects I have been suffering with occasional attacks of fever and ague, and a very sore mouth; in fact, so bad is it at this present, that I can hardly eat a slice of mashed yam. My principal food is eggs, when a good one is obtainable. It is a peculiar custom here not to allow a female to eat an egg, it being the prerogative of mankind only to do so; from my over-partiality for this kind of refreshment, the ladies often call me, sarcastically, "the fowl-egg eater."

As a matter of course, the reader will not be surprised to hear that I have again been robbed, the article being nothing more or less than a small carronade which had been stationed in my yard as a defence. Why it should have been preferred to three belonging to Akia, all lying in the yard, I am at a loss to know; but probably my suspicions may be well founded—they are these:—

My sagacious predecessor, much to his credit, allowed five of Ajie's niggers to build and occupy huts upon some of the factory ground. The chief of this gang, one Obue (like master like man), is Ajie's spy; but having carried on his systematic plunderings successfully, he has become a petty trader, and not being contented with small profits, he made away with one of his master's bullocks (as well as four goats belonging to me), and that master having no regard for the saintly precept, "Do unto others as you would they should do unto you," seized upon the person of Obue, who, like a true penitent, confessed this instance of his manifold sins and wickedness, but at the same time purchasing his life by promising to obtain a suitable recompence for the wrong inflicted upon so proverbially kind a master. From these facts, I incline to think that my carronade is to form a portion of the promised recompence.

10th.—Purchased a quantity of oil at a good discount this morning about 9 A.M. Just as I was about concluding the work of the day as I was wont to do, a cry of "thief" was raised. I whisked out with revolver in hand, aimed, snapped the trigger, but the cap misfired; and though it is as dark as pitch, the son of darkness is seen rushing into the bush which surrounds the house. Really, I think the greatest curiosity to be found in these parts would be an honest man. It would require a second Diogenes and lantern to find out one; but Aboh is ruled over by brutality, and its aristocracy (faint not, ye nobles) maintained by plunder.

Midnight, and I am still up and alone, pacing the house to and fro. The pestilential dew is falling, and yet the protection of the factory demands the exposure of my life. Really, no payment would be equivalent to the daily sacrifice of rest; no, not for any amount would I spend my time here over again, unless I had efficient and competent aid, to mitigate, if not to share, my anxiety. Here I am, my eyes bloodshot, and my body in a perfect fever, and for what, I ask again. No judicious man would leave another in such a state. Perhaps to-morrow I shall be sick and prostrated. I hope to God that, should this fall into the hands of my deluded successor, he will pay attention to himself, or he may have to bear the ills peculiar to this God-forgotten race and land. I am too excited to revise this entry.

12th.—Prince Akia called upon me to solicit an advance of goods to the value of a ton of oil, promising at the same time to pay me within a stated period, and furthermore to place a slave in my hands as security.

"But should this slave die, shall I lose my oil?" I asked.

"Oh no," was his answer. "Should he die during my absence, you must cut off one of his hands, and retain it until I return, and I would make the amount good by payment or a fresh security."

I advanced him the goods, knowing well that I should be paid, and that if much longer on hand, they will be stolen or useless.

I have great satisfaction in observing that my security is very contented; so much so, indeed, that he would like his master to linger in the payment.

13th.—A trip to Onitsha, by the author and five Nigerians.

"Upon the lake of life we glide."

After a great deal of fuss and bother, I managed to engage five men from my fast friend Tschukerma, on payment of two pieces of satin stripes, the total value of which was 2*l.* 10s. 4d. Well provided with stock, that is to say, rice, yams, &c., I chartered a canoe, and embarked in state for Onitsha, the distance from here being about forty-five miles, and the trip upwards occupied us four days. I can assure you that being rocked to sleep in such a cradle as my canoe was anything but pleasurable, considering the discontented state of my bowels. Then, again, comes the unsophisticated blessing of luxurious repose upon some (till then) untrodden ground. There may you loll at your ease, and of course you must submit to the eccentricities played upon you by the mosquitoes as best you can. Poor things! how they buzz about you, singing you to sleep with their strangest of strange lullabies, evidently composed in honour of your visit. And if they do alight upon your person and inflict their sting, you are amply recompensed by knowing that you are in the Niger; and without a few peculiarities of a similar nature, an African voyage would be anything but singular.

My time and passage was profitably employed, for I was picking up crumbs of information from the memories of Jem Bunt, and really I should have been an object of pity had I been without them, for Morpheus is my evil genius, and the mosquitoes, aided by the sand-flies, waged war against him, and fought out the contest upon my body.

Fancy, dear reader, laying yourself beneath an African sun in the day-time, and cooling yourself in the dew-dropping night-shade.

During my passage I called upon several mighty kings, and from one, Orissa Buma, who dwelt at Oque, I received a goat and some yams, all of which I gave to my people. They sat up all night preparing the repast; thinking me asleep, they showed their brutal propensities, which they endeavoured to hide from me, in the dressing of their food. The goat was taken and partly devoured; stupified and helpless it was thrown upon a pile of burning timber. I arose and upbraided them for their cruelty, but their reply was a question.

"Massa, you na' rufie?"

"No!" I replied. They thought nothing further of the affair, but with one fell swoop commenced the discussion of the goat. I was disgusted with the sight; the animal could not have been upon the fire above twenty minutes, and yet it was pronounced done to a nicety.

On the morning of the fourth day we espied Onitsha, and I must say, as it now appears, it is a very pleasant situation. My steward, Tone, showed me

"A sweet and shaded nook."

Here I divested myself of my travelling suit, and commenced my morning's ablution, and I can affirm, upon my veracity, that there is nothing half so sweet in life

"As bathing in a stream."

Just as I was getting along with my toilet,

my attention was arrested by the appearance of an English long-boat approaching my verdant dressing-room. Glad enough was I to see it. I hurried my clothes about me, and just appeared ship-shape (though only half trimmed), when she came alongside. My visitors were all coloured men, but of a superior class, the first and foremost being Mr. J. C. Thompson, Mr. Laird's agent at Onitsha, by whom I was most cordially received. He thereupon related how he came to observe me.

"Look," said he to Romaine the pedagogue; "there's a fine bird."

"Yes," answered Romaine; "have a shot at it."

Thompson was about to take aim, when he observed Tone bringing me a red shirt. Immediately he put his boat about, and at length discovered the white man's distinguishing pennant, that is, a large red umbrella, abaft the binnacle of my canoe. Well, thought I, my life is not insured, and what would have been the result had I been fired into? (many would say killed or wounded) but Providence, I thank thee for guarding me so well. After exchanging compliments, Mr. Thompson informed me that he was going to visit the King of Oko, and would be pleased would I accompany him. Despatching my canoe to Onitsha I entered the boat, and after a short pull I paid my first visit to

OKO.

To reach this town at low water, you must ascend a perpendicular height (exceedingly pleasant to a body corporate), and when you have managed your ascent, you may then steer to any point you choose; but I can assure you that the Okonites, one and all, are the dirtiest set of people I ever met with, so much so that I could not help uttering—

> "Go away, black man,
> Don't you come anigh me;"

for I was teetotally sickened, both by men and matter, both of which you may find in plenitude rotting 'neath the sun. Our first call was made upon the village blacksmith, who is a very ancient man. Ah! there he sits beneath a bamboo shade, blowing his charcoal fire with great solicitude. His bellows, though rough and rudely constructed, are not without ingenuity; I will endeavour to describe them. Two hollowed pieces of wood, with tubes attached, are sunk in the ground, and are built around with mud or clay; over these tubes is placed a sheepskin covering capable of being expanded; to each of these skins a wooden handle is attached, and when worked up and down like a slow-moving pestle, a strong current of air is forced through the tubes. This man is what Patrick would christen a "janus," being laureate, actor, musician, and major-domo to his Royal Highness Prince Buma, the reigning Lord predominant over the Ant Hills of Oko.

Our next visit was to his princeship, whom we found squatting on a mat, robed in a tattered shirt of many hues. Both his eyes were bedaubed with chalk, but as this is the prevailing fashion here, I took but little notice of it. In answer to his wishes, I seated myself upon a leopard skin beside his highness. Then came rushing in the élite of the township,

> "Maidens fair and young (and very dirty),
> With sweethearts hale and strong;"

and with them came a numerous fraternization of piccaninnies, who, upon seeing me, would set up a beautiful screaming-match, to which was added a species of original acting by the lady mothers. His highness presented me with a goat and three fowls, at the same time intimating that he was very poor (gentle hint for a "dash"); but calling to memory his visit to me, his complainings waxed weaker. I obliged the nobility by quaffing some palm wine, and then we left. Lord, how the women and children ran away before me as they saw me approach. On every side my ears were greeted with the cry of "Tschuko" (*Anglicè*, God). We proceed onwards, and successfully make our descent once more in the boat, and after many hurrahs and strong pulls, we arrive at

ONITSHA, OR LAIRDSPORT.

The landing-place or wharf at this place is a small extent of sandbank, bounded on either side by grass and brushwood; it is rather steep, although not tedious to ascend.

Up we go, and onwards through a grove of mighty palm and pine; at the extremity of which we discern the factory, a mud-built house standing within its own enclosure. It is here where many a ton of the finest palm oil is purchased. Ivory as yet has not obtained a favourable footing, owing to its scarcity.

After partaking of a most comfortable meal, we began to talk over business, &c., and, after a glass or two of grog, we turned in. I cannot help mentioning that I slept but little that night, fancying every moment that I was in my canoe, and that the least movement would capsize her. I had the pleasure of reposing on my back until I reached the sacred land of Nod, unacquainted with that pernicious animal the nightmare.

> "Oh, sweet it is indeed to rise,
> And greet the morning sun."

This morning being my first here, I

availed myself of an invitation given to me yesterday by Mr. —— to visit the Mission-house and schools. They are situated about a mile from the factory, and on the town road. Though the distance is of the shortest, I really felt it very tedious, on account of the excessive heat. The road we traversed is a straight one, lined on either side by millet, grain, cocoa, and the famous cotton-plant, two or three samples of which I plucked, and a very pretty production of nature it is. Mr. Thompson, who accompanied me, very kindly informed me of the mode of its cultivation.

We at length arrived at the Mission-house, or houses—for there are three of them—one of which is in the occupation of Messrs. —— and ——, the others are intended as the future residence of the Rev. Mr. Taylor and party. There is also a very roomy schoolhouse. A word now about the labourers, viz. Romaine and Smart. Romaine is a native of Sierra Leone, and is, I believe, by trade a stonemason. He came out here as a steward, and secondly became a petty trader, that is, to be trusted by the factories with goods to a certain amount, and in return he is to pay the value in palm-oil, or other produce, at a marketable price. How he has succeeded is not my business; suffice it to say he is now the Onitska schoolmaster.

Smart is a native of this vicinity, but spent some years in Sierra Leone, where he came to the knowledge of Christianity and its wonders. He is very aged, and I think from his appearance that he needs repose. His white hairs command respect, and he ought to be most liberally pensioned, for I am given to understand his services have been full of faith and manifold. I was extremely pleased with him, and it gives me great pleasure to bear testimony to his good teaching. About eleven of his school-children came forth, and saluted me with a bashful "Good morning, sar," and curtsey. One little girl was extremely interesting, and as she looked up to her mother (also a member of the school), who stood by her side, with eyes ripe with expression, and watched me very closely, I could almost fancy that she wished to ask—

> "Mother, where do white men dwell,
> On land or in the sea?
> Or do they live in heaven there,
> In mud-built huts like we?"

After spending an hour or so, we took our leave, at the same time inviting Mr. Romaine to take a cup of tea with us. We retraced our steps, and once more sat down out of the calid sun. We then set to work and heartily partook of an excellent dinner. A walk was proposed, and carried to the length of two miles or so. After enjoying the beauties spread out before us we returned homewards, ripe and ready for any mischievous merriment, and, after a pleasant evening, retired to rest.

Arising by first cock-crow, I made active preparations for paying my final visit to the Mission-house for the purpose of ringing the bell, inviting my friend Mr. Thompson to accompany me. He most willingly consented. About nine o'clock we started, and by twenty minutes past we arrived. Upon entering the portico we espied Mr. Romaine, who greeted me somewhat sullenly. Mr. Smart was in a merry humour, and a relation of our jokes last night drew from the poor old fellow many a token of merriment. Palm-wine and nuts were then presented, of which I freely partook. After a stay of some forty minutes we rose to depart, and hen I rang aloud the bell, much to the surprise of the villagers. Hastily wishing success to the missionaries, we left, and an hour afterwards I was on my way to Aboh.

Mr. Thompson having business at Oko, I went in his boat, my canoe following in our wake. Arrived at Oko, I met with a degree of respect I had not anticipated. It seems that several Abohonites to whom I had given a dinner on Christmas-day were there before me, and repaid my kindness by calling me loudly Isama Okpae (*Anglicè*, Child of the Sun), and bowing to the ground, they finished their exhibition of respect by giving me a charm called a juckanjie. It is composed of a small piece of wood, and covered with strips of a yellow metal. It is usually worn suspended to the wrist, and is supposed to render all imprecations harmless. Mr. Thompson and I then paid our respects to the king; after so doing, I set off in my canoe, sensibly feeling my first trip to Onitsha. Towards nightfall I came to harbourage at Ohvos's'so, the principal palm-oil and slave depôt in the Niger. Here beneath the falling dew I pitched my tent, or mosquito-bar, and here I lay to await the coming of a foggy morning.

Toward midnight a party of slave-dealers sought me out, and importuned me to purchase seven slaves. I expelled them indignantly, at the same time intimating that I bought palm-oil. They replied that they knew that, but why would I not buy niggers? To this question I gave no reply. My visitors, seeing it useless to plague me, departed.

I am now in the centre of barbarity and slavery. It is here that flesh and blood is sold, and will continue to be sold as long as slavery exists; in fact slavery, in many cases, is a blessing, and not a bane, as many would infer. I'll be bound to say that a slave here is not so oppressively treated and taxed as our own unpitied artisans. I say artisans, for he must "first procure his hare before he can cook it;" and whilst these devils (pardon me) are lolling in laziness, debauchery, and filth, even the most humble labourer in England may work for food and taxation. What has been done for our own countrymen in comparison to what has been, and is doing, to ameliorate the sufferings of the so-called unpitied negroes?

Let a few philosophical philanthropists come out here for a short time, and I'll be bound to say that they will learn to take care of their bullion for the future.

It is an old adage, that "Charity begins at home," or ought to do, and it is likely to remain so, with so much folly afloat. Spend no more until we know that our own people are properly clothed, fed, and educated, and then the social position of Africa will have abler resources to call upon. What in the name of heaven have we received from Africa to balance the annual waste of men, money, and material? Have we received a vote of thanks for all that has been done and established? From personal experience I am enabled to say that ingratitude, the worst of all sins, is our reward. How many homes have been rendered desolate and void by the sacrifice of fathers, sons, and brothers in the furtherance of civilization? Certainly we are sacredly ordered to teach, but after we have taught, should not the pupils be able to strike a blow themselves for their own emancipation? But no; these ungrateful fellows hesitate not, when gain lies before them, to murder and to mutilate their benefactors. I say ingratitude has hitherto, and ever will be, nine cases out of twelve, the white man's reward. Talk about civilization indeed! do not the promoters in many cases seek

"A bubble reputation"?

And I here declare that centuries must elapse before slavery will be lessened; and moreover, lives, and many too, will have to be wasted in an attempt to circinate Africa.

Here is an extract (an old one truly, but none the worse for that) forcibly detailing how one portion of our sweated taxation is expended:—

"FACTS CONCERNING THE SLAVE TRADE.

"It is impossible, perhaps, to give an exact estimate of the sums of money which have been expended by this country in the attempt to suppress the slave trade. It is highly probable that twenty millions sterling have been devoted, first and last, to this branch of public service.

"There is not only the direct expense incurred by the cruisers which have been employed on the coast of Africa, the West Indies, and Brazil, but that which has been paid to foreign powers to secure their co-operation, the expenditure in and for Sierra Leone, the Gold Coast, and Fernando Po, bounties paid to captors of slavers, salaries to the mixed commissions, pensions, &c. &c.

"According to the latest estimate, the charge for the suppression of the slave trade is stated as follows:—

Vessels on the West Coast	£291,501
And for vessels not exclusively employed on the coast	£414,953
	£706,454

Exclusive of the sums paid to captors, mixed commission costs, &c., probably the amount expended is more than £1,000,000 sterling per annum."

So vast an expenditure on ineffectual

efforts to suppress this hateful traffic, clearly shows the impolicy of the measures hitherto adopted to secure that end.

But to this enormous expenditure, let there be added the annual loss of life, as far as practicable, and I can assure my fellow Britishers that they would turn their attention homewards. Here, the people are strong and fond of filth, and, as slaves, they are happy; but divested of their bondage and left self-dependent, we have proofs to certify that they will die of filth and starvation.

Without breakfasting, I ordered the canoe to be pushed off, and once more we were afloat; at half-past five, P.M., I landed at Aboh, just in time to witness the conflagration of one part of the town.

The following being a specimen of female life in the Niger, I shall offer no apology for its introduction.

It is, and ever has been the fashion in this part of the world, before a girl arrives at the age of puberty, to entrust her to the care of a masculine member of her family, who, upon assuming the responsibility, has to present his ward's parents with an expensive "dash," or present, as a proof of his unalterable friendship; he has also to swear before his gods and fellow-men, that he will return her pure and undefiled. Should he fail to do so, he is compelled by public voice to repay an ample recompence for the girl's dishonour; this penalty, in the majority of cases forms the marriage portion of the injured lady, who then becomes the wife of the highest bidder; and thus the buyer claims his bargain. He generally pays her intrinsic value in cloth, cowries, sheep, or bullocks, and the price is regulated according to the social position or standing of the parties. But should the gentleman fulfil the terms of his oath and agreement, he then becomes an honour to society, and in return receives an ample reward from every one concerned; is voted a "brick," and is thus enabled to glide through life respected and revered.

The following is verbatim, being a literal translation of what my sable heroine kindly sat down and narrated to me. Whilst so engaged, she repeatedly asked me for what purpose I was noting her words; I briefly told her that I intended it for my people's information.

"Ah, ah," she sobbed, "the white men will then know how they make us slaves. Banna akpoe banna" (*Anglicè*, "Child of the sun, thank you, thank you.") Thus she began—

I was but twelve years of age, when a youth made bold to woo me I was pleased with his addresses, and consented.

My parents were next consulted about our marriage; they smiled, and as is customary, demanded the financial proof of his esteem; it was granted, and I was laden with favours and presents. A year hence was to see me his consort, and I quitted my parents' roof for a residence at Lawrien, one of the principal Zourba towns. Here I was located until fitted for the wedded state, when I again sought the home of my sire. The night preceding my nuptials, I was sauntering alone, when Masābă, the notable chief, saw and seized upon me. By him I was taken to his palace at Laddu, and placed for safe keeping in the hands of the chief mistress of his harem, until the time the Mussalussĕ (or Mahometan prayer-meeting) was over, when he would return and marry me. During my captivity, my betrothed discovered my whereabouts, and hastened with the intelligence to my father, who immediately set out and begged for my release, but he was driven forcibly away. My betrothed, upon hearing this, seized upon an individual belonging to a different tribe, declaring that he would hold him until my liberation was effected. Masābă, upon a knowledge of this, sent my intended a substitute for me, but he refused to accept her. . . . . The identical morning upon which the feast and prayer-meeting was to have been celebrated, a civil war broke out, and the town was fired. I effected my escape, and after many vicissitudes I arrived footsore and jaded at my father's house two suns (two days) afterwards. My future consort appeared and again claimed me for his wife; but alas, alas, the morrow's sun shone upon his corpse, for he had died of poison. A few days subsequently I accompanied my father to Igbegbe upon a trading excursion. Here I was demanded as wife for the Dowdoo, or head-man of the town, but my father refused, preferring to bestow me upon the brother of my betrothed.

One evening, shortly after sun fall, I was walking alone upon the sand beach, when I was seized upon by the Dowdoo's people, who transported me to Oko Kaie, about a mile from Iddah. My father again sought me, but his approach being heralded, I was hurried to the Rialto where merchants most do congregate, and then I was sold; the payment made was salt and rum. On the morrow I was brought down to Aboh. My father, I believe, is dead.

The subject of this memoir is still to be found hereabouts, and the veracity of her statement has been verified by one of my traders, who has spent several years at Igbegbe, the scene of her early struggles.

January 29th.—The cause of my visit to the town on this occasion was to inquire into the motive Akia had for not returning my canoe, the loan of which I had granted him some two months ago, but which, despite of several messages demanding its restoration, was not forthcoming. I thought my personal interference would effect my purpose, therefore, calling for my horse, I mounted, and, attended by my assistant McCauley and my interpreter Tom (who could, by the way, utter some fourteen and a-half words in English), rode over in quest of Akai. Upon entering the town, the first place of note we espied was the residence of Ajie's eldest son Orissa (worthy sire, worthy son), which is, like every African tenement, an erection of mud and sticks. I noticed hanging by the tail a huge catfish, not in the least unlike Barnum's mermaid, as a jue-jue. This was before the grand entrance. Before that of an inferior department was also hanging, but by the horns, a goat's head. I do not know, nor will I pretend to say, that it was emblematical of what had been discussed at dinner, for such a thing as a goat (unless stolen, when it is eaten to avoid detection) is never purchased by any member of clan Ajie, I conclude therefore that it was used as a fetish. So much for the entrance of the town. Now for a peep inside, where your olfactories may be regaled with the exquisite delights of a hundred stenches; really, I am obliged to put my Rosinante s mettle to the test to escape suffocation. What with handkerchief to my nose and the beastly groups around me, I can assure you I was not a little pleased to find myself in front of Akia's residence, which is situated in the centre of the town. Here I dismounted, and, giving my charger to the care of a gentleman who made no direct demand for thus obliging me, I entered the mud-built palace of the prince. After a tedious promenade through mud and bamboo sticks, I entered a courtyard where, seated beneath a shade, I found the object of my visit. Near him was seated his son Archar, a boy of some seven summers; a little further off reclined his chosen mistress, snuffing up the wind and sandflies, and wallowing like a sow in laziness and filth. Akia, the richest and most haughty trader hereabouts, was robed in a cotton tobe, and was surrounded by the élite of his private pandemonium. A chair was produced, and I sat me down at least two feet higher than royalty itself. After the usual salutations, he ordered in the wine (the luscious extract of the palm), which was as sour as vinegar, wherefore I drank but little of it. I soon opened the purport of my visit to him. He replied that he had entrusted my canoe to the safe keeping of one of his slaves, and having heard that I had threatened to make him pay me three puncheons of oil for it, he had the man put in irons until such time as the canoe could be found. I asked to see the man. My request was granted, and I was ushered into a small back yard, where the prisoner lay upon a heap of excrement and other refuse; his legs were fettered to a huge block of timber. So disgusted was I that, after a few words, I promised to procure his liberation, for in him I had on several occasions found a friend, and in accusing him of the loss of my canoe, I had every reason to believe Akia had told me a lie. I again therefore sought the prince, and demanded freedom for the serf, as a test of friendship. After a brief but very spirited palaver, the man was ordered to be released, and a deuce of a row was created during the unfettering of the wretch. However, in half-an-hour the prisoner appeared, and fell prostrate before his master, exclaiming—"Banna mŏdĕ, banna" (Thank you, master, thank you). Akia then told him that it was to me he owed his gratitude, for he could refuse me nothing. In conclusion I thanked Akai, and christened the man Downcast, by which designation he will henceforth be known. To give him a chance for self-advancement, I engaged him for the factory, and, upon receiving a promise of the speedy return of my canoe, I left.

Leaving my horse in the hands of Downcast, I walked over to the palace of the tyrant Ajie, whom I found alone in his glory, his body literally covered with chalk—in fact, he was actually too ill to groan. After a brief *tête-à-tête*, I left him a prey, as he must be, to a thousand reflections. My next call was upon Tschukerma, whom I found ably discussing with his lady the peculiar delights of their vesper meal of dog's-flesh. I was offered a platterful, but finding illness a sufficient apology for refusal, I offered it.

In fifty minutes afterwards I was safely located within my factory.

31st.—It had been my intention to have visited Oguānĕ to-day, but the chiefs of that town and this being at daggers drawn, I must defer my visit until some coming day.

February 1st.—Towards eight o'clock, P.M., the usual guns were fired from the factory, to warn stragglers that after that hour all visitors would be treated as thieves, and, as such, liable to punishment. "Poking a smipe" very leisurely, I received pantomimic sign to be on my guard, but without waiting for further information, I seized my revolver and cautiously stole out. After a search of some time I saw, or thought I saw, a faint shadow gliding away at a rapid pace, and somewhat suddenly descend into a pit. Overgrown as it was with weeds, it was the work of some moments before I could bring my optics to bear on the penetration of so dense a bush. However, I succeeded in finding the shadow, and handcuffing him. A light having been procured, I was not a little surprised to find that my prisoner was the identical individual who had stolen the carronade before alluded to.

3rd.—Master Ajie sent his butler to visit and to cheer up the prisoner, who was charged by his master not to be dispirited, as active measures would be taken to effect his liberation.

Prince Akia, accompanied by his son and a retinue of some fifty ragged noblemen, paid me a visit, but their stay was of the shortest, and of little interest. About an hour or so afterwards, the watch guns were as usual fired, when Downcast made his appearance, and gave me a hint or two. Apprised of villany abroad, and Tom and the cooper having been sent into the town by myself, and not having returned as yet, I sent for McCauley, who with myself were the only two about the premises. Arming ourselves, we went forth, when Mac immediately saw a figure moving in rapid advance of him. He pulled the trigger, but the cap misfired, and the game for a time was lost. A few steps further another movement was observed, and I aimed, but with no better success, for my pistol was in the same condition; and, to mend the matter, I had but three other charges of ammunition in the whole establishment. Returning to reprime my piece, I cautioned McCauley as to the advisability of his changing his attire, for as he was at present very conspicuous, I thought it would be better for him to assume, as near as possible, the garb of the native. This done, out we went again. Presently I observed a figure sneaking somewhat rapidly away. I fired, and with some effect, for a stentorian voice proclaimed its owner to be wounded, and blood was afterwards discovered upon the spot.

My next thought was the store, which, to my chagrin, I found broken open, and a considerable quantity of property strewn about the ground. The amount of goods stolen I estimate as over 40*l*. Nearly the same amount was piled together for immediate conveyancing. However, nothing could be done until the state of affairs had been reported publicly to the chiefs of the town.

McCauley having proceeded in quest of information, espied a gentleman coming hurriedly from the bush, and immediately change clothes with another party, evidently on the alert. Upon learning the features of the fellows, McCauley returned to me, in company with the cooper and Tom (just returned). Acting upon impulse, we all set out, and seized upon the individuals. In endeavouring to do so, one of them attempted to stab me. This was sufficient; a scuffle ensued, the result of which was I captured two persons, and had them bound heavily with hoop iron.

I may as well state that I possess but one pair of handcuffs, and yet I have two madcap bravos to look after.

After a night of suspense and anxiety, I sent Tom and the cooper to acquaint Tschukerma and Akia of the robbery, and to demand their presence at the factory.

About nine o'clock a party of gentlemen, some of whom were connected with last night's depredation, assembled in my yard, armed with guns, matchets, assaigais, and even bows and arrows. Upon my asking what they wanted, I was told that they had made up their minds to kill me, and seize at once upon the property. A general oath was then administered, the purport of which was that I should not live to see the sun go down. Upon this I walked into the house and armed myself; my two men acting similarly, and following in my wake, were ready and even eager to obey any command I might give. The first order was to shoot any hostile person seeking an entrance into the house; unloaded guns did as much service as loaded ones, for each was looked upon as an instrument of death, and had the effect of silencing the enemy, who retired sagaciously to await fresh orders from Ajie, who was himself too cowardly to appear, and thus overpower me. Presently Tom arrived, attended by two men from Tschukerma and two men from Akia, and bearing with them a request to me to bring my prisoner over to them, that the case might be clearly investigated. I tarried not, but giving myself into the hands of God, I ordered the first prisoner to be left in the charge of the four men alluded to before, and my cooper. As I have before mentioned, I had but one pair of handcuffs; I was forced to leave my first capture without a bond, further than a palm rope, the handcuffs being required for the safe conduct of the man to town.

After a hurried walk beneath a most glaring sun, we arrived at Tschukerma's house, where I found him awaiting my coming; he offered me a seat, upon which I fell, for I was too exhausted to stand; he then saluted me, which I returned. Here we sat, he scrutinizing my countenance with evident concern and awe, so much so that he exclaimed, "Some one will die to-day;"

to which I replied, "The day is young as yet." Akia by this time was announced and presented to us. After a brief palaver, I addressed them rather briefly to the effect that I was the only white man in their town, and as I had been most unmercifully robbed by Ajie and his people, I demanded their assistance and protection.

Akia then rose up, and in the name of his brother, politely requested me to lay my complaint before Ajie in person, and return to them with the tyrant's answer. Upon this hint I acted, and straightway repaired to Ajie's domicile, where I found him undergoing the operation of bleeding (he can well afford it, for he has bled me pretty freely), and seated in the midst of his harridans. Around him likewise congregated the elite of his pandemonium, for he had heard of my being in the town and bearing arms, and felt rather unwilling to meet me. But I had taken him by surprise, therefore he was bound to rise up and greet me when I entered. Never did fiend look so fiendish; his very eyeballs as they dilated seemed illumined with satanic lustre, and fain would I have struck him to the earth for his villanies; but he held out his hand, which I most reluctantly took, to hide the hostile feeling in my thoughts. Salutations over, I laid my complaint in full before him, in answer to which he said—

"How long is it since you have called to see me?"

"That has nothing to do (seeing his disposition to change the subject) with my present visit; all that I want from you is redress for the wrongs you have inflicted upon me."

Ajie then said he would give the men the poison-nut to drink, so that they should not rob me again; but before he could do so (hereupon he smiled upon the assembly, who of course smiled in return) I must present him with two gallons of rum, two pieces of cloth, two guns, and two kegs of powder.

I told him flatly I would not give him a gun-flint. "What!" said I, "you set your niggers to rob me that you may be fed, and then you have the damned impudence to demand payment from me for so doing?"

"Well," said Ajie, "I am the King of Aboh (a pretty king and kingdom) and Tschukerma is my brother. I alone built the factory, procured the sticks and levelled the sand, and for so doing I have never been paid."

"You are a liar," I replied, exasperated; "you have been amply rewarded."

"How do you know that?"

"Your brother and my books are evidences of the fact."

"Well," said he, "I will call the men." It must be observed that he wished to call forth the men before I had pointed them out; it will be obvious therefore to my readers that he was privy to their depredations.

"Do so."

"Will you give me the cloth and the rum if I do?"

"Not a gun-flint."

He then sent for the men (the very thieves); but during the absence of the messenger, my cooper came running towards me, and related that half a score of Ajie's slaves had entered my house, released my prisoners, and had beaten him (the cooper); and to conclude the matter, they had sworn to burn the factory down.

"All right," said I, advancing to Ajie's front, and producing my revolver. "Set fire to my house and you are a dead man."

His sable majesty shook again, fearful

that I would anticipate their intentions by killing him outright I then walked out, saying I would soon return and confront the bravos.

"Where are you going to?" he exclaimed.

"To ——."

I then hastened over to Tschukerma and Akia, to whom I related the success of my mission. After a draught of palm wine, I again sought Ajie, whom I found seated behind a huge wooden bowl, containing his meal of dog's flesh and chillies; he partook of this merely out of bravado, for had he not done so, his wives and compatriots would have called him cowardly. The men soon arrived, and Ajie called them forth, and wishing me to repeat my accusations, I did so.

"Have you heard what the white man has said?" asked Ajie.

"Yes, sire," they replied.

Ajie then placed his head upon his right

hand, heaved a heavy sigh, and very feelingly told them to depart and rob no more.

Rising hurriedly, I said, "This, then, is the justice I am to receive, and certainly it is as much as we ought to expect for coming to such a God-forgotten hole; but remember, Ajie, I will one day meet you on equal terms, and then we shall settle our long account. Until then, be kind enough to inform those of whom you are the master, or progenitor, that should I catch any one of them near my factory I will shoot him." I then left him; his wives, concubines, and niggers generally, retreating in every direction. So much for Ajie. I could wish him transported to the hottest of all regions; but alas, the devil

> "Will not have him damn'd,
> Lest the fat that's in him should set hell on fire."

I then sought Tschukerma and Akia. After a rest of some few moments, and a glass of palm wine, Akia rose up and began a very long rigmarole concerning his brother's rascality; but while doing so I could not help thinking that he (Akia) would as soon impose upon me as anybody else. Therefore it was that, without mincing matters, I appealed to Tschukerma for two men to act as watchmen, to which request I received a most polite and ceremonious answer, to the effect that I should have four men, two from himself and two from Akia; and should they (the men) give me any cause for complaint in the slightest degree, death should be awarded them. The kola nut was here demanded, and brought forth with many expressions of kindness and goodwill towards myself.

I then left Aboh (I did not expect to do so, for I had sworn to die if occasion demanded it), and hurried towards home—oh, happy word—which I reached pale and careworn; for I had been under the influence of a most calid sun for the past seven and a half hours, with no other covering than a felt hat. Just as I was about to seat myself, Ajie's steward, who had evidently dogged my footsteps, came running up to me. The reason for so doing was obvious, for he had a dagger in his hand; but I rose as if to meet him, and he took to his heels.

I cannot bring this day's work to a close without recording my gratitude and thanks to my assistant, McCauley, and my cooper, Jos. Blenkinson, both of whom most effectively and nobly aided me throughout this most troubled day. Had it not been for them my journal and career would have been concluded; therefore let me reiterate those glorious words of Crabbe—

> "The fondest and the best,
> Are those most tried, most troubled and distress'd."

From the date of my last entry, we have

been suffering most acutely the effects of starvation; many days our whole subsistence has consisted of and depended upon a roasted yam. Meat of any description is not to be obtained. Talking about meat, I may as well insert the following ludicrous affair which took place last Sunday.

About three o'clock in the morning I heard a gentle tap at my window, and rising up I questioned the rapper as to his business. He replied very softly that he wanted to see me. I admitted him, when to my surprise he informed me that he had brought with him a fine monkey for sale, and hearing that I was hard up, perhaps I would buy it.

As to water, we have plenty, for we are forced to drink that of the river, and of beastly waters, the Niger beats them all. From the combined effects of this and of the living, I am so reduced in frame and vigour that I cannot move about unassisted. In such a situation, it is no wonder that the African trader should give a sigh for England.

"His home, sweet home."

Many of my fellow-traders have felt the same, and do not blush to find it known.

February 18th.—This morning, scarcely had the dawn appeared before the reality of the fiendish Ajie stood before me. We neither greeted nor saluted each other, but I requested my men to be upon their guard. I then walked in and closed the door of my principal entrance, thus leaving Ajie and his serfs and servitors outside. He had come with his people to remove some salt belonging to him. I had allowed him the use of several puncheons in my yard to stow it in, and now he came to pay it away for some slaves which he had just purchased in front of my premises.

Meanwhile he ordered some twelve of his attendants to take his barbaric mess of a breakfast into my dining-room. On a previous occasion I might have consented to the proceeding, but in this instance his gross ill-treatment spurred me on to give him a blank refusal. On which an entrance was to be forced, but firmly resisted. Ajie by this, thinking he was losing caste in the eyes of the traders who were with him, arose to exert his authority, with sixty sable devils in his train, armed with pots, pans, porringers, pikes, and pistols. At this time I was reclining in my hammock, being, as I have before mentioned, very weak. Advancing rapidly upon me, he seized me by the throat. Taken unawares, and so helpless too, it was most fortunate that McCauley was near to unhand me. Feeling any further resistance to be next to impossible, I sought my bed, at the same time telling Ajie that as I was now about to enter my sanctum, he must not think to enter, for I should be prepared for him, and one of us must most assuredly fall, for weak as I was, I had yet to learn to act the coward. I now left him. Upon this Ajie swore he would slay me; seize upon the property, and burn down the factory. He was about to set the example when his eldest son Orissa (*Anglicè*, God), came up, and sent a private messenger to me to bid me remain quiet, and he would pacify his father; however, it took a long time to do so, for he had sworn to kill me, and kill me he would. He then took a fearful oath, calling upon his defunct sire to wither his limbs if he did not slay me before the setting of the sun. Upon hearing this, and knowing that my existence is of some little value to a certain maiden of my acquaintance, I determined to defend it for her sake. Calmly (for presence of mind is essential) placing my faithful Colt in my belt, I appeared before him and bid him do his worst; if we had quarrelled, we only ought to fight. So abruptly had I answered him, that his fiery temper was somewhat cooled. In the course of five hours he had paid away his salt, and as I had another puncheon in my hands as security for some oil he owed me, and which, after a good deal of palaver, he had paid, I wished him to take it also away, and such request meeting with his entire approbation, I unlocked my store door and ordered the salt to be given up to his magnanimous self. Upon seeing it he would not receive it, alleging that it had been disturbed, and some of it stolen. And such indeed was the fact; for some of his slaves having a short time before broken into my store, in their hurry and excitement incautiously took away some of it, and which act they had not thought it prudent to acquaint their master with. The loss, as I told him, he must certainly sustain, but I left it optional with him whether he removed the remainder or not; and when the ship came we should come to a proper understanding. Ajie, upon this, expressed his royal intention of staying in the store until I produced the stolen salt. To this I replied, he was at perfect liberty to do so, but as it was getting late, I would thank him not to keep the door open longer than convenient. His majesty then uprose, expanded his chest, coughed once or twice, and finally told his followers to seize me, but they had smelt powder before, and therefore displayed some reluctance to obey the royal command, which, being observed, he ordered them to remove a puncheon of oil belonging to me. I bid him stay a little, but he insisted upon its instant removal. Seeing it about to be carried out, I was necessitated to declare my full determination to shoot any man, the king included, who should attempt to molest my property. A consultation was now held between them, and the removal of the salt was finally agreed upon. He then rose majestically and hinted to his people that "the smallest donation would be thankfully received;" upon which several commenced a pilgrimage of theft, but they were followed by the sagacious Downcast. Ajie then to crown the day, called all his serfs around him, and made each and every one kneel and kiss his largest toe, and swear by his body that they would slay me upon the first favourable opportunity. If I was seen in the town, they were to seize upon me and bring me to him, and he would perform the pleasing operation of scalping me. "Yes," said Ajie, "under his own roof the gods say we cannot kill him; but when he is under the canopy of heaven then he is unprotected, and his life is forfeited." He then left me, to my great satisfaction, for I had not tasted anything since his arrival, and feeling somewhat hungry I proclaimed the fact aloud, and Downcast set before me a dish of exquisite yams.

March 18th.—Added to our present hungry condition, the Abohnites seem determined to strip as well as to starve us. In the present instance, I am the only loser. It must be understood by the generous reader, that I, being a responsible agent, no wonder will be manifested at my day's work, consisting of twenty hours out of the twenty-four on an average. Well then, after a very hot day's work, as usual I felt somewhat sick at heart and weary, and for repose I sought my bed, and shortly after I was in the fond embrace of Morpheus, realizing to some extent that

> "Sleep is pain's easiest salve, and doth fulfil
> All offices of death, except to kill."

About midnight I awoke, and judge my surprise when I beheld a breach large enough to admit a good-sized body, which had been made by removing the soil in which the posts supporting the house bad been planted. Many of the posts being rotten or worm-eaten, and my not being rich enough to furnish better ones, aided the burglar very materially in his exploit; but whoever he was, he must have been a fellow well acquainted with the house. After an examination, I discovered that I had lost my watch, chain, trinkets, and almost every stitch of wearing apparel; in fact, I had none other than the shirt and trousers I had slept in to appear in, until McCauley's ingenuity fabricated me a pair of "sit-upons" out of a sack.

In the afternoon Akia sent to inform me that Ajie was in possession of my watch, cap, and suit of clothes. For the information I returned my thanks; but as I had found a dagger in my room belonging to the thief, who had intended, no doubt, to have used it if necessary, I was very much concerned as to the ownership. I have my suspicions, but will allow time to mature them before I make them known.

Tschukerma, upon hearing of my loss, kindly sent me a felt hat.

5th.—Ajie will not be contented until he has committed some irreparable mischief. This morning a company of slaves belonging to him assembled and began parading very ostentatiously in front of my factory, and continued to do so until they were driven away by the excessive heat of the sun. Impatiently I waited to sift the matter, but seeing no other chance, I set Downcast on the watch, and presently he returned with the glad intelligence that Ajie was determined to consummate his villany by shooting me to-day. He had issued his mandate to that effect. My body, alive or inanimate, was to be brought to him. I was to be slain privately, openly it durst not be done, for their moral creed and doctors say that it is not lawful to kill a white man before the setting of the sun; after that hour there is no restriction, further than the shielding arm of Providence. However, matters soon assumed a different aspect, for a slug came whizzing past my head. The hand that fired the shot was in hiding. Again the savages assembled, and to such extremity did they carry their bravado, that I was compelled to resort to stratagem to defeat them; therefore, calling my people together, I hurriedly told them to arm themselves, for at this juncture my situation was truly deplorable. Here was I, and two coloured men, about to face some two hundred savages of the deepest dye. However, I had my flag hoisted, and with the feelings of one who has never met a coward or a slave beneath it, I headed my people with the firm intention of fighting or falling. But neither was done, for the bravos fled before us, nor do we think that Master Ajie will dare to attack us so boldly again; if he does, God give us strength, and we will teach him a lesson. But the worst of such matters is, that when Ajie plans his villanies he sets deputies to execute them, which leaves us no other alternative than thrashing his niggers, to whom life and its loveableness is as foreign as their desire for Christianity, unaccompanied with grog and blankets. However, it is to be hoped that the work we have begun will be accomplished unsparingly by those whom fortune has driven forth to battle with the world.

In a peculiar, if not a melancholy mood, I retired to rest, but being unable to propitiate the sleepy deity, I arose and extemporaneously ground out the following:—

"Oh, I am sad, yes, very sad,
As how can I be gay;
When friends and children living are
Far, far away.
Yes, yes, stern solitude has found
In me a son sincere;
But happy is the man who has
A maiden to revere.

I love the mountain, rugged, wild,
The ever-smiling sky
Is all the canopy I ask
From man or Deity.
I look not for life's solaces
In other than a tear;
But happy is the man who has
A country to revere.

Upon the rising surf I mount,
And stem the curling wave;
Where men in numbers have before
Been hurried to the grave.
And yes, I smile when current thoughts
Of dangers passing near,
For happy is the man who has
A safeguard to revere.

Pagans are my neighbours now,
And yet my mind is free
From other hopes than loving God
And bright eternity.
Yes, I have seen the heathen kneel
As penitent, sincere,
And happy is the man who has
Religion to revere.

I've seen some human bodies fell'd
Upon the open plain,
Mactations they to mortal man,
To palliate a pain.
And yet such sights, so common too,
Are dreadful and severe,
For one who has a "native home"
And kindred to revere.

I've dwelt in peace, in pride, in pomp,
I've sat down with the poor;
But now I find experience is
A solace and a cure.
For every ill a man may bear,
Though life be sad and drear,
Is yet to live, to feel, to say,
Contentment I revere.

Now for my pipe, my most favoured panacea for all complaints, both mental and bodily.

6th.—About forty canoes left Aboh, freighted with slaves. It would be a profitable undertaking for any man-of-war's gig to enter this river about this time, but for a vessel of tonnage I would have it ascend about the latter end of June, or early in the following month; and as the river begins to fall in October, it would be advisable to be prepared to descend at that time.

9th.—This morning, Tschukerma, in company with his brother Ori-bou-du, called upon me, and pressingly invited me on board of their canoes. After so doing, I had a meal prepared for them, much to the gratification of Ori-bou-du, it being the first time I had so honoured him. At the conclusion, Tschukerma offered up his thanks in a very affectionate manner, and retired; but in the course of an hour or so they returned, bringing with them several large yams and four pots of palm-wine. I then called for kola-nuts, which I presented to my guests, they repeating the following:—" Dissie af-ya efa-rerebere. Watta emarefe-egga-bere efe demi bere Tuko abierma. Ohshimri bata-ge eshe-bawom eshe batru-um. (Blessing, good trade, plenty of food. Have patience with small things; wealth in store. God be with us. Let the river flow in peace; no headaches, no stomach-ache.)

After so doing, the wine was sent round until its potency began to operate upon the faculties of the princes, when they again arose, and saluted me a gŏ-mhor, or God, declaring that I should never die; but should Ajie kill me, might my body resume its wonted animation in my mother country; whither it is supposed the spirits of the dead white men and those of the defunct Aboh kings resort for repose. I felt it incumbent to disturb these fanatics by mounting Tschukerma upon my horse, and sending him home to his lady wife; the other prince, after a deal of bother, was prevailed upon to enter his canoe, when he, in a state of somnolence, was paddled away.

11th.—We experienced a very heavy tornado about eight P.M. My house was partly unroofed, and my cooper's dwelling completely blown away.

16th.—To give my readers an idea how my generous friends Ajie and the Abohnites punish the crime of adultery, I will here relate an actual scene of which I was an eyewitness.

Ajie, be it known, professes to have about sixty wives, ranging from the tender years of ten to the harridan of fifty. All of these he compels to attend upon him, and to maintain themselves, for he feeds them not. Many of them are petty traders, but the profits arising thereby being small, they are necessitated to prostitute their persons for food, and to supply their lord. The guilty persons on this occasion were one of Ajie's poorest wives and one of his head slaves, a man whom Ajie ought to have revered, rather than have punished, for it was through him that he was able to aspire to and maintain the throne of Aboh. It was the cowries of this slave that had purchased Ajie food and clothing, but, as I have often said, ingratitude has its motive. So it was in this case, for Ajie's motive was to rid himself of his many obligations, for he was under many to the object of his brutality, and to obtain possession of what little wealth the slave had by stealth accumulated. Having occasion to wander abroad, that is to say, as far as the grave of Dr. Batchelor,

I was greatly surprised to hear my name pronounced aloud, and the frightful sounds of the kaugai, or drum, falling on my ears. I hurried onwards, and was met by some forty individuals, escorting between them a man whom I well knew, and of whom I have bought some puncheons of oil in my time. I advanced, and made bold to inquire the cause of this excitement, which inquiry Ajie was pointed out as capable of answering. However, I took all in good part, and remained a silent observer. Ajie presently began a long oration, eloquently touching upon the enormity of the culprit's crime. His matchet, or rather an ugly carving-knife, was brought to him, and Ajie (the brute) began to divest the man of his ears. During this operation the assembly were chanting and yelling most lustily. A plate was called for, upon which were placed the culprit's ears. Rum was now brought forward and distributed. Ajie then proceeded to rip open the poor fellow's abdomen; this over, the platter was again produced, upon which was placed the lower members of the murdered man, who sank groaning upon the turf. He was immediately bound to a stake, with a stick passed through his body, and sent down to the beach, there to be propped up as a warning to all future transgressors of the seventh commandment.

The woman was compelled to eat the portions of her paramour's flesh.

I am writing this in my dining-room, and I must say a bleeding corpse is anything but a pleasant object to have before your window; however, I must have it removed.

On my return from witnessing the death of the poor fellow before-mentioned, I was disagreeably surprised to find a numerous assembly of Abohnites and other members of the brute creation, congregated together upon the beach, whither I proceeded in quest of information.

The scene before me is anything but pleasing, though the sun has cast his amber mantle over the tepid Niger, and a gentle breeze is blowing to cool the calid air. Around me stand about twenty or thirty athletic negroes with a worn-out canoe of goodly size as a centre piece. A sacrifice is about to be performed, but a very harmless one; for Akia is about buying a new canoe, and as its owner lives at Oru, he, Akia, is about to send a deputy to arrange as to the purchase; but before he sets out, a sacrifice must be performed to make the affair a lucky one. Amongst other things I noticed a goat, a wild fowl, fish, pepper, &c. Whilst I stood beside Akia, he with his own royal hands killed the goat and sprinkled some of its blood upon the canoe, at the same time walking round and round (like the witches in Macbeth) and uttering aloud the following mystical words—Beko-beko Wăde. Na ja af-fear satu wade Naja Abasu ju gum abor. Mado Na-guire muta zou naja. Beko-beko satu cum-ja cum bere. (Do, do, master. Going to market. Softly, master. Going to Abasu to buy a canoe. Men tell me that you refuse. Do, do. Softly let me go and return.)

We then parted; I with my eyes a little open, and Akia with the full conviction that good had been done.

18th—After the affair of the day before yesterday, Akia discovered to his chagrin that he had been victimized by one of his wives and a slave, and as the man through fear of detection had destroyed himself, and thus disappointed Akia of his revenge, the sale of the wife was next proposed, and she was sent down to Oru to be sold for rum. Before setting out she was ordered to array herself in her bridal costume; to wit, two yards of fancy cloth round her loins, one yard of silk round her head, and one string of coral to ornament her neck. Thus appearing, she was seized upon by her faithful sisters, who beat her well and drove her with curses beyond the town without a rag to cover her. The sale was soon effected, for she was a comely woman, and Akia and his concubines made merry at the expense of her unfaithfulness.

23rd.—Ajie, as a matter of course, is celebrating the sacrifice so recently committed by him.

29th.—This morning a lady from Oru, accompanied by a fine female slave, craved my permission to allow them a seat in front of the verandah; which of course being granted, they presently began a performance of which the following is a description:—A pot was brought, into which was thrown some charcoal to be pounded; the elder woman then began drawing upon the back of the younger one some rude but very pretty outlines in chalk. The device was rendered permanent by being cut into the flesh with a peculiar three-cornered instrument of native manufacture; the blood of course flowing copiously from the cuttings, was stanched by the aid of the powdered charcoal. I must say that her beauty was not heightened by what she had undergone (though two or three months hence her back will be like a piece of embossed morocco leather). She is a perfect charmer of an African, and as she stands before me (though naked to the skin), with a bright brass chain slung very negligently over her bosom and shoulders, I cannot help thinking "nature unadorned 's adorned the most."

April 6th.—The fellow whom I have

introduced to my readers under the name of Downcast has greatly incensed me by his ingratitude. Ever since I had taken upon myself to become his patron and task-master, I have done my duty. First of all, it will be remembered, I released him from captivity, and since then I have fed, clothed, and, when sick, have doctored him. But really, the spirit born within him began to assume an unwonted callousness, and the following result may be taken as the average reward received by the white man for such kindness and protection. Has it not been said that all are moulded alike by nature? If it be true, I feel convinced that nature was drunk when Abohnites were born.

Yesterday, this individual stole a goat belonging to his most excellent majesty Ajie (and as I had lost two about the same time, perhaps it was but tit-for-tat). The goats had been left in the hands of Obue, one of his highness's most obliging bravos. The animal was slain, and a portion cooked for me, of which I ate a very comfortable meal. I do not mean to insinuate that I was privy to the theft, but being on the verge of starvation I ate till satisfied, and of course asked no impertinent questions. The lost goat haunted the mind of Obue, who durst not upon any account visit his royal master. He then privately waited upon my assistant, McCauley, and told him confidently that he had lost a goat and that he was convinced that my men had stolen it. This was duly reported to me, and in reply I told Obue to find me the man and I would make good the theft. After a lengthened and a fruitless search, although it was thief catch thief, he returned and craved permission to see me, which I granted; and strange to relate, he begged to inform me that if he could find the thief who had stolen the goat, he would tell me who it was who had entered my house some time back, and stripped me of my clothes, watch, &c. I then politely told him to speak the truth, and I would give him a piece of cloth. After receiving a dozen bannas (salutes), I showed the gentleman out. The morning came, and so did Obue, attended by his suite of bravos. My men being in attendance, I had them confronted, whilst I stood watching closely each physiognomy. Obue then laid his charge, which being unanswered, he flatly charged Downcast with the burglary before alluded to. Downcast became, in truth, cast down. He admitted the theft, but denied all knowledge or participation in any robbery committed previously. To which Obue said Downcast had told the truth, for he (Obue) and his companions now before me were the thieves, and in many cases they were compelled to do so by order of their master, Ajie. Ajie, he said, was in possession of my watch, cap, and other items, and he had made them into jue-jues.

I then handed him the bribe, and dismissed the gang. Upon this I sent McCauley to Akia, the owner of Downcast, with full particulars written upon paper, and insisted upon a judicial hearing, and three puncheons of oil as the value of my personal property. The day was very wet, and Akia expressed his surprise (and well he might) at my message, but he had already received a full account of the palaver from his "Own Correspondent." Akia treated McCauley haughtily, and sent him for Downcast, who on hearing that his master had sent for him, departed with much consequence and bravado. In about two hours he was sent back to me, pinioned, and under an escort of six; his body, especially his breast, bore evident marks of the bastinado. Upon facing me he fell prostrate and yelled most furiously. Akia's messenger then addressed me:—

"Aĭkwa (Child of the Sun), my master sends this man for you to kill; will you do so?"

I replied, "I do not want the man's life, but I do require ample restitution for my stolen property."

The messenger then produced about two fathoms of cloth and a few loose beads, saying—

"The man has confessed having robbed you of these, but refuses to reveal more, and my master (for the second time) wishes to know whether he is to be killed."

I again repeated my refusal to have the

man murdered, but should my request have any weight with Akia, I would not sanction the release of Downcast until he disclosed the names of the receivers of the stolen property. Upon this Downcast, seeing no loophole to escape through, made an effort to gain the river, which meeting the approbation of the bystanders, I thought proper to have him brought back, and re-sent to his master with my compliments, for the manner in which he had endeavoured to make up for my loss. I have since learnt that Akia has filled Downcast's eyes with pepper to make him speak to the truth, but as yet he is not susceptible of any impression.

As I have mentioned this as one case of ingratitude, I offer no apology for the introduction of another.

I asked a native of Sierra Leone who is eating at this present time the white man's bread, and whose parents were made free by British valour, and made capable of earning their livelihood by British money, whether the profits arising from the discovery of the Niger would ever compensate us for the loss of life experienced thereby? He replied, with the grateful grin of an African, "Who asked the white men to come out here? Why did they not stay at home? Did we send for them?" So much for African gratitude.

8th.—This morning Ajie sent his son to lemand from me a puncheon of oil, as the value of the goat stolen. He also informed me that the goat was *enceinte*, and as it was likely it would have increased his stock by three at the birth, he should also expect an equal value in oil for them. I agreed to pay him, providing he would also pay me at the same rate for those stolen by Obue from me at his instigation. Since then I have not been annoyed.

10th.—This day I had an opportunity of talking with Ali Hairie, poor Lander's servant and interpreter; but what I elicited from him in desultory conversation does not differ materially from what is already known to the world.

20th.—Up to the present date nothing worthy of note having transpired, I made up my mind, in answer to many entreaties and polite invitations, to pay a visit to the town of Aboh the less; for it must be understood that Aboh is divided (I have said so before), and two scoundrels (Ajie in particular) usurp the monarchical authority. These fellows are powerful, and love murder and rapine with a gusto befitting only monsters. Nana Sahib, of Cawnpore notoriety, is no bad idea of what either of these chiefs would be, if their power was unlimited. However, with their brutality we have little to do at present: therefore to my theme.

A VISIT TO ABOH MINOR.

Having been fortunate enough to elicit the profound approval of my neighbours for curing them of several maladies at one time very prevalent amongst them, it is no wonder that my name became as familiar in their mouths as an household word. On many occasions I had been importuned to make a call amongst them, but as often have I strenuously refused to do so; however, upon this occasion I allowed myself to be persuaded, not merely to gratify them, but as a relaxation and a palliative for my own monotonous existence. My escort consisted of about twenty of the élite of this Shibberdegallian tribe, and my interpreter Mousad. Towards the close of the day we started. Our road lay over the sun-scorched beach, and as we wended onwards our attention was called to, and greeted with the incomparable beauties of an African shore. The margin of the river was loaded with many a gay and sportive specimen of the piscine tribe, whilst, as a deeper border, the towering palm in dignity raised its head, and bowed in kindly recognition to the broad but feeble plantain. In vain has the ebbing tide rushed in fury for years, endeavouring, as it were, to compete for further dominion; but no, the wise prevision extended to all things by our bounteous God has given to each enough, and yet no more. Upon every branch, be they of palm, the plantain, or the pine, we discern the playful inmates of the bush; in fact, what with the chatterings of the monkeys and the music of the feathered flocks, we had enough entertainment to cheer us through a wilderness. A few strides bring us before a small expanse of water, as clear as crystal, and formed by nature into a pleasant creek, where, upon its breast, were floating the canoe of the slave and the state canoe of the negro Rothschild, laden each and every one with produce from afar. Here do we find the diminutive piccaninnies importuning their *maters* for that sweet nutriment mothers alone can give; while others, as the case may be, are dabbling in oil or rolling in the sand. How happy must they feel in their unsophisticated life! Their pleasures seem to find a gusto in their insignificance. Every possessor of a loin-cloth, a pipe, and a pot of oil, is in himself a king, and their vocations, be they respectable or otherwise, are prosecuted to the utmost, until they become the possessor of a wife, when she is bound to keep the man in luxury, if laziness be called a luxury; and often, in furtherance of that object, she becomes lost to morality, and sinks into her grave a prostituted being.

After a hurried survey of the immediate scenery we proceeded onwards through a lane bounded on either side by luxuriant corn and yam fields. Presently we discerned another expanse of water, but this time it is a placid stream, rushing gently past a row of dilapidated dwelling-houses of the poorer class. Before us stands the ferry-house, a bamboo-thatched shed, and in it is seated the ferry-man, who rises at our approach and politely offers for the customary fee of five cowries to paddle us over the water, not to Charley, but to Aboh Minor. This done, I made my first call upon my patient, who seemed to be a dropsical old fellow on the verge of seventy. Here I sat me down and listened to his complainings, and, had I not displayed some unmistakable signs of impatience to be gone, it is not improbable that I might have been there at this present, for every question put by me was answered with a groan. Beating a retreat, I proceeded onwards to a grassy plain; deeply shaded was my path by the hanging foliage of some thousand trees, until I arrived at the mansion of my friend Buma Pĕrĕ, who, unfortunately, was not to be found; but my presence was greeted kindly by his sixteen wives, all of whom I found in the occupation of making fue-fue (mashed yams and water). Here I seated myself, and smoked a pipe or two to amuse the ladies, who quickly surrounded me, whilst the favourite sung me a plaintive ditty to a drum accompaniment. The other ladies could not sing on account of their strict adherence to the Nigerian fashion of snuff-chewing. I proposed a dance, but this could not be done, owing to the immense blocks of ivory in which their shins were encircled. I have on many occasions noticed on the shins of the Aboh and Onitsha women circlets of ivory weighing from twenty-two pounds, as a mark of their worldly distinction. However, a walk was suggested, and as there was a festival to be held not a hundred yards off, I allowed myself to be escorted thither Five minutes brought us to the scene of mirth and meeting. The ground was certainly not overcrowded with vans and vehicles, and the numerous indispensables of an English fair, but black and buxom were the damsels congregated to celebrate the demise of one Tschukerma, who had departed this life ripe with years and bullocks. It had been his desire when living, to be followed to heaven when defunct by ten of his most faithful and willing slaves, and this was proclaimed aloud by the executor, who stood with hands upheld and loudly called for the assistance of the son and heir of the deceased, who quickly came, and appeared anxious for the sacrifice to take place. Accordingly, a yell of joy proclaimed the news, and three bullocks were brought forward and felled; then were brought the ten human victims, who were beaten to death, and their corpses buried with that of their master. Yes, the very grass seemed eager for blood, and yet enough had not been spilled. Another victim was to be offered, but my heart was sick and satiated, and I was resolved to stay no longer; but a female being brought forward, bound and fettered, I stood aghast, whilst the poor creature, with glistening eyes stood terror-stricken. Upon this, my better nature predominated; I interfered, and offered to ransom her by giving the butchers a fair marketable price for her. My overtures for a time were disregarded, but rum being wanted to complete their mania, my price was taken, and I had the gratification of receiving the female, and finally removing her from the fate that seemed impending. She was happy; but so sudden was the change, that for some time I thought she would have swooned away. Still, kindness did its work, and I am proud to say she has lived to thank me in numerous ways. By this incident the reader will be enabled to find how much human existence is valued in the Niger. With a sad heart, I returned homewards; making towards the stream, I was accosted by several gentlemen who urgently invited me on board their canoes, but I positively refused, and on I went. Presently I came up to a gentleman who stood mounted upon a sandbank, shouting loudly that he had lost his salt, and presenting a small calabash filled with clay, chalk, cowries, and a colouring pigment. He begged his god, inhor, or devil, to follow the thief or thieves and return unto him; but, if unable to do so, might they (the thieves) be damned to all eternity. After a smart walk, I reached the factory; but judge my surprise when I found that my footsteps had been dogged by a female trader, who in company with her husband and child had followed us onwards. She here related to me that Azakah's son had seized several kegs of powder, guns, and cloth, and that she could not recover them. She had heard that I possessed charms and medicine, and she would pay any amount to learn the result. I plainly told her that we had but one God, to whom alone all things are known, but she would not believe me. Seeing a pack of cards upon a table, she seized them, and said they were my inhors, to which I jestingly replied, "Yes, they are; and if you will do as I tell you, I will consult them for you." I then began to shuffle them, and presented the pack to her for her to choose one whilst I should cover my face. She did so, and for better recognition, she showed it to all around her save me. I then bid her place it in the pack again, and to her astonishment the chosen nine of diamonds was reproduced. I then told her God would decide between her and Azakah's son. She stood perplexed, and ejaculated in the Aboh language "Oebo be Tschuko" (*Anglicè*, White men are gods). She afterwards departed, promising to return to-morrow with a goat as a sacrifice to my God; and verily, say I, when it does come we will have a feast.

Towards midnight a great hubbub was heard, and the cause I elicited was, that a sister of the young king, Oko (who is now here) had been kidnapped. Upon hearing which he headed his people and set off in search of her. How the matter ended I do not know, but when I again met them she was nearly broken-hearted.

24th.—Our present starving condition renders it almost imperative for me to say—

> "'Tis feast we want, not fast, ye sinners,
> For our great fast is want of dinners."

Such is my situation that I am compelled to despatch my native labourers upon a begging expedition. For the last five days my subsistence has been nothing else but rice and cocoa, a strange mixture, certainly; but with an occasional yam, stewed in palm oil, we manage somehow to exist.

This is Sunday, and we are without a mouthful of victuals, save what my friend Tschukerma has sent me in shape of dog's flesh.

25th.—This morning hunger forced me to arise and set forward with my gun for the purpose of obtaining some bush meat; and after an hour's rambling I returned with a monkey and a parrot. These, when dressed and cooked, will form no despicable meal.

27th.—Tschukerma paid me a visit, accompanied by a long retinue of his ragged nobles, who had for the want of something better to do, followed him to the factory. Before leaving, I prevailed upon them to do some little work in the shape of repairing my salt store. Whilst in the act of conversing with the chief, a report as loud as a thunderbolt fell upon my ears, and, to my extreme dismay, a portion of a musket barrel whizzed in fury past my head. By what miracle I was saved I know not, but by the providence of God my career was not ended. I picked up the splinter, and had the party who had fired it taken as he was about to make off. Tschukerma having heard a long rigmarole of a story, ordered the fellow to be well flogged, which of course was immediately done. From what I am given to understand, this is but another instance of Ajie's attempts on my life.

30th.—This day I had an opportunity of witnessing the native mode of obtaining potash, the first part of the performance consisting of making the charcoal. This done, water is poured upon it, and the sediment allowed to fall into a tub, which being left to stand, is found to contain ashes little inferior to our own. This is gathered together, and is sold in quantities at a very remunerative price.

It may seem strange to my readers to know that the Abohnites have, or profess to have, but four days to the week—

Akă, the first, or Sabbath,
Orĕ, the second,
Aphor, the third,
Ungor, the fourth,

and consequently fall short of ten months

to the year. From actual observation I learn that they begin their months upon the appearance of the moon, .and not before. Should you ask a negro his age, he will look at you, and recurring to some event which happened about the period of his birth, will probably tell you he is some hundreds of years growth; but you may be enabled to solve the mystery by dividing the number of years given by twelve, as by that number of moons we calculate our own year, the quotient obtained being the number of years he may have seen.

May 18th.—During last night a very heavy tornado was encountered, and the rain fell in torrents; in fact, the ground was completely deluged, and the wind was so furious that when I arose this morning every item bore the signs of destruction. The very outhouses were denuded of their roofs. In fact, many of the building-posts had been shaken with such effect that it occupied us above an hour to reinstate them in their former condition.

Even Ajie's goats had to find shelter and refuge in the empty puncheons, and, to my extreme surprise, one was found dead, probably through fright. The people of England can form no idea of an African tempest. My tenement remained firm, although the rain found its way through the roof of thatch, and a miserable sight the interior presented. Outside, here lay prostrate uprooted trees in profusion, completely impeding the progress of man by their ponderous arms; there lay the wreck, or disjointed staves of many a cask, arranged in the nicest confusion by the elements.

I am now surrounded by the niggers belonging to Ajie's chief mistress, A-mer-ric, with whom I have just bargained for a puncheon of the finest oil that I have had the good fortune to meet with in this river. Her ladyship having been met by one of my labourers who was wheeling a barrow for the purpose of conveying gravel to the factory, and she being struck by the novelty of the thing, entered and seated herself, and was trundled in state into my yard amidst shouts of joy and admiration. I immediately advanced and offered my arm, an action that was not lost sight of, but was repaid by a "dash" of two yams and a pot of palm-wine.

May 2nd.—This day a man called upon me, and earnestly entreated me to give him some medicine. Upon asking his complaint, he placed his foot upon the table, and exhibited, to my disgust, the absence of one of his toes. He told me that it had been gnawed away by rats, and as this is a very common affair, I felt no disposition to disbelieve him. Giving him some advice, and a smaller amount of lotion, he went his way. *Apropos* to the above, I have been suffering for the last fortnight with an ulcerated leg, likewise a very prevalent contagion, and my stock of medicals being so small, I have concocted a lotion or liniment of opodeldoc, goulard lotion, and a little blue-stone dissolved therein. Whether or not this is a true course I do not pretend to know, but suffice it to say that it seems to do me good, and perhaps it may serve as a bit of advice to my successors. The rats are very numerous in this part of the world, and are of the largest size. It is not unfrequently that my little house-boy has arisen suddenly in the night, and, rushing to me, shown his hand, and often hands, streaming with blood, the effects of the nibbling kir-ru-coes. Even beneath my own mosquito-bar, I have to build a regular wall with blankets, &c. to keep these nocturnal visitors outside. What with rats, thieves, starvation, and illness, a man must be a perfect Job to keep his temper. I never felt the bite of a rat, but those who have, have informed me that they give a nibble, and, should it disturb you, they will soothe the pain with even breathing upon it.

3rd.—Sickness is very prevalent in this district; no fewer than ten aristocratic Abohnites have left this world for another since yesterday, and the town is in a perfect furore on account of the numerous sacrifices that must be offered in the course of eight days to celebrate the death of the great, and for the rising of the river.

May and June are the most sickly months that a European can experience in Africa, both months being the heralds of the rainy season, with its malaria, fevers, ague, dysentery, and an innumerable lot of diseases peculiar to this nation. No man can be too cautious as to what he may eat, drink, and avoid. Fruits being plentiful, I would advise any European to have as little to do with them as he would wish to have with a native, without the chance of obtaining produce. At this time I have found it highly essential to keep the natives at arm's length, and when within a stride of them, I generally puff a weed, and so drive the stench of their uncleanliness before me. Being rather cold at this time of the year, the Africans rarely resort to the water for the purpose of washing themselves, but having a nice idea that filth keeps them warm, they suffer their skin to assume the cast of leprosy and emaciation. For the last month I have not observed six cleanly persons in the town of Aboh, the royal brood included.

4th.—Still raining, and the ground has become so muddy that I have not been outside the house for four days, but a messenger from the town called, and informed me that the Abohnites were to arm themselves and proceed to Oh-qua-rue for the purpose of resenting an indignity which the tribe of that town had hurled upon the Abohnites. Ajie and the rest of them are to appear upon the battle-field to-morrow.

THE JUE-JUE ISLAND.

On the other side of the Jue-Jue Island, (a small rock rising in the very centre of the river and facing my factory, so called by this superstitious race), the God of the Sea (be it known that they know not of the ocean), is worshipped, and here is the table upon which they sacrifice both man and beast at the shrine of their paganism. I have on many occasions noticed upwards of five hundred pilgrims dabbling in the blood of their victims, and discussing the virtues of their several gods. Heyday, what a sight it is to see canoes arriving from most parts of the Niger, laden with their living freight, either for the slaughter or for penance, just as the fit may take the chief of the party, who, should he be armed with a petty authority, will not fail to outstep the bounds of modesty or manhood; and when they do assume their savage wont, woe to the ears of the European, should he be at all anxious to hear the yells of the butchers commingled with the groans of the dying. Then, again, to give a zest to these disgusting scenes, the musician thumps away at his drum until the temper of a Job might be raised to such a pitch that the saints would damn him to all eternity, and perhaps kick him out of their society.

It was a beautiful afternoon, the sun was fast declining, and the cool air of evening was about to waft away the heat of the day, when I ordered my canoe to be got ready so that I might visit the sacred island. Everything prepared, I set off, paddled by four lusty fellows, and in the short space of ten minutes I set my foot upon the rock, and wandered over the place, and even trampled upon the buzzard-picked corpse of a man until I was heartily sickened of my visit. But as the least endeavour will bring us some reward, I gave the order to paddle to the other side, and here I met a sight well worthy of my visit, and were I but a painter or artist I would have made a sketch of it, and have tendered to the poets a theme worthy of their praise; but as I am neither a poet or a painter, the African trader must be allowed to describe the scene in his own way.

Wending onwards, I struck into a secluded path-road, beneath the shade of the most gigantic trees that ever graced a forest. Beneath my feet lay trampled a fragrant bed of weeds, excelling by far the beauties of many a dearer stem. Persevering on my way, I at length espied a timid rivulet rippling on its course with its gurgling of song. Upon the bank stood a tenement, lonely and desolate to all appearance; but after a strict scrutinization, my impertinence and curiosity excited the anger of an ancient man who came tottering onwards, leaning upon a staff for further support. After saluting the old gentleman, our conversation began, and to such an extent did it reach, that I not only learnt his history, but that of his occupation. He informed me that he had been a slave, and had suffered slavery in his youth, but when manhood came, so did his sense, for he has cut his eye-teeth. Knowing the superstition most prevalent, amongst his tribe, he invented new ones, and became in course of time the mhor or devil of the town. If sickness prevailed, he was sought to cure it; if it rained too frequently, he was sought to decrease it; and *vice versâ.* Cowries came in plenteously, and he prospered; but having prognosticated to a woman that she would give birth to twins, and that prophecy having been fulfilled, he was ordered to be sold, but ran away no one knew whither. The woman, on the other hand, as is the national custom in such cases, was driven out of the town, and her children destroyed.

Time elapsed, and our hero found his way here, where he has reared his own palm, built his own house, and, for the convenience of his visitors, grinds corn, tells fortunes, and is a professional ascetic. To his numerous avocations one more has yet to be added, and that is a kind of Gretna

Green establishment, where a woman can get married without the trouble of wooing. Now this very respectable old man is of a robust make, well-formed, intelligent, perhaps too cute, and seems to enjoy his health. Before his door he has apportioned to himself a plot of ground, upon which he rears his vegetables and live stock. He lives alone, to all appcarance, but he has an assistant, and never allows himself to be seen. Any pilgrim visiting his threshold must first hold palaver with a skeleton form who acts as his double; and for advice, which he fails not to give, a regular scale of charges is laid down. But if you are rich, he leaves it to your generosity, and before departing, which you must perform backwards, you must leave the deposit or payment upon a block of stone, from whence it is removed and added to the store of this miserly old fellow.

He expressed his satisfacation at having commerced with Oeboe, I being the first he had ever been near to, though he had watched the progress of our vessels, and by so doing discovered our colour. Just as I was about to depart I heard the hum of a dozen voices, and asked for information, when I was told that he must now depart, for his children had come to wash. Waiting a few moments, a female drew near, bearing a bag of clothes. Her features were well known to me; in fact the bag was mine, in the hands of my washerwoman. I soon solved the mystery of their approach, which was for the purpose of washing themselves and clothing by this old brook stream, which being more private, and more free from oil and filth, is generally resorted to for such purposes, and for dancing on its banks by "de light of de moon" Unabashed by my presence, they fell to work. I may visit the ascetic again, if possible, when I hope to be able to glean a little more concerning him.

I have just heard that old Tschukerma's people have been fortunate enough to kill an antelope. If such be the case, I make no doubt but I shall have a glorious feast, and the hope of it must be my excuse for saying so.

5th May.—Ajie and his brothers, with their amalgamated troops, left Aboh for the purpose of fighting in earnest; but after half a day's work they considered it more prudent to rest themselves, which they did, and, I believe, cooked also. Perhaps I shall know the full particulars to-morrow; so I, like them, will rest myself, for my leg is so painful that I am forced to lie down, and of my knees I make my desk; therefore my log for the day is so much shortened.

6th.—My leg is much better, but I am

still unable to move about without some assistance, and the weather being so rainy, I feel the want of creature comforts most acutely The temperature is so very cool, that I am forced to wear an overcoat to keep the cold out. I may as well mention that Master Obue and company resumed their wonted avocation of thieving last night; but luckily they did not visit me until this morning, when they came with several barrels of oil, all of which I bought unsuspectingly. Towards four o'clock I heard a loud voice issue as though it came from the beach. Taking a stick and the arm of my assistant, I tottered towards the same direction, and met a person, evidently in a great hurry, and bearing in his right hand a string of cowries and a calabash of medicals; in his left he carried a matchet, both of which he raised suppliantly to heaven. I was interested with, and watched his movements, the next of which was stooping to the ground and filling his mouth with sand, which he retained for some moments, and then spat it out. The fanatic then resumed his course onwards, and in a frenzied manner entreated the string of cowries and the calabash to lead him to the robber's den, and point out the party or parties (none other than Obue and company) who had stolen his oil. Should his search be fruitless, may the pilferers be apportioned with hell. The victim stood for some time before Obue's hut, but knowing that Ajie is his master, he thought twice before entering, and when he did he was severely handled by the gang, who would, had it not been for me have added insult to injury. This is the general mode in which the Nigerians make known their losses, and endeavour to recover them. Poor creatures, they have yet to learn the utility of a county court.

I have just learnt that the Aboh troops have returned crestfallen, though some of the nobs are glorious with victory. The Ohquarnians not deeming the Abohnites a worthy tribe, declined to fight; but like peaceful citizens, carried on their business unfearful of interruption. There is to be a great feast in the town to-night. Every reputable person is bound to send a tribute to the slaughter, and an item of wearing apparel to propitiate their go-mhor (a god or pagan deity), who is supposed to exterminate the most prevalent diseases. Would that I were well, I should be there to see and likewise notify.

7th.—I experienced this day the greatest shock that ever fell to the lot of man before. The early part of this morning I toddled, as is my wont, to inspect my premises; entering my palm-oil store, I discovered a being in the greatest agony. His body stank to such a degree that I was forced to cause a log of timber and some grass to be burnt to cleanse the air. He presented a form of rottenness and filth hardly conceivable; every part of his body was covered over with ulceration, and the fetid matter running in streams from the various sores, turned my stomach completely sick. The poor creature was even void of his loin-cloth. I learnt that he had been an opulent trader, but having been ill, he allowed an Aboh Jue-Jue man to administer medicine to him. After a useless waste of money, he was turned out incurable, and by Ajie's orders was driven out of the town. Suffering great agony, he managed to crawl into my store with the calm intention of dying, for his cure or recovery seemed hopeless. Upon my entrance, the wretch managed to kneel and salute me, entreating me not to remove him. His condition being past my aid and comprehension,

I ordered him some food, which being brought, he ate so ravenously that ere he had consumed the greater portion, he fell backwards, groaned heavily, ejaculated Banna, and breathed his last. I cannot but think that he died of a broken heart.

It is a fashion peculiar to the Nigerians, more especially the Abohnites, should they see a fellow creature suffering from any sensible disease, first to ascertain his wealth, and should he be wealthy, it is extracted from him (generally by Ajie's order, who, as chief of Aboh, claims his portion, which is generally the lion's share) by the go-mhor of the town, who, after so doing, mutters something or other, and leaves the victim to his fate, which generally ends in death and a coffin of matting (*i. e.* should he be such as to be entitled to this consideration), in which he is consigned to the river, to become the food of alligators and the other inmates of the Niger. It is very pleasant to know that we are forced to drink this water. It is no unusual sight for me to witness the transportation of the miserable bodies to their watery grave. Life here, is a commodity to be bought and sold, and regulated according to your value. Should you be a free man, and possess a dwelling-house, you are buried within it; but should you be a slave (or a nigger as the term goes) you are consigned to Fishmongers' Hall, for the benefit of the struggling piscine race.

I have just heard that Ajie's mistress, Anazoe (the identical harlot who caused the victim killed by Ajie to be sacrificed), has again fallen into error by transgressing the seventh command of our Lord, and her husband is on the *qui vive* about it, declaring that they shall both die, *i. e.* should he be fortunate enough to entrap the man; but meanwhile she is to be sent to the bush, and forced to live in privacy.

9th.—My life hitherto has been a mixture of smiles and tears, but to-day I enjoyed a right jolly laugh; and prithee listen, gentle reader, perhaps you may enjoy the same.

My friend (a friend, ye gods, in a region like this), Prince Arroboudoe, of happy memory, having been sent by his most satanic highness and brother, the gentle Ajie, to Egarrah upon a trading expedition, by some' mischance managed to lose some seven slaves belonging to Ajie. Fearful of encountering the tender disposition of the beloved, he failed not to institute a very vigorous search after the fugitives; but mercy on me, he was unsuccessful, and with careworn visage he returned home. Rumour had carried the news on before him, and Ajie received him but coldly. An investigation took place, but could not be brought to a finale until further proofs had been obtained. In the course of three days one of his majesty's spies, ever on the watch, discovered to his surprise that one of the runaways had been sold to a Brass trader, and hastened with the glad intelligence to his master, who immediately sent for the trader and for the slave, both of whom duly appeared, and were thus interrogated—

"Where did you get my nigger from?"

"I bought him," was the reply.

"Who sold you?"

Arroboudoe was pointed out by the slave as the seller; upon this a tremendous yell was raised by the audience, who, though very anxious to declare the prince guilty, could not do so when he declared his innocence and offered to procure ample testimony to clear himself. This being prudent and satisfactory to the elders, he proposed to again visit Egarrah for the purpose of escorting Ajie's son, who was bound to the place in search of evidence. They started, and after a brief stay they returned to-day, their canoes in full trim, and under the command of Arroboudoe, who stood at the bow, blowing a huge cow-horn with such effect as to make the sounds the avant-courier of his arrival and innocence. When he jumped upon the beach, he and his niggers set up the most hellish chorus that ever dinned the hearing of man. His next performance was to lay himself upon the ground, and suffer himself to be rubbed over with chalk; when he arose, a most ghastly and peculiar sight presented itself. The grease upon his body having rendered the chalk moist, he looked like a dirty chalk figure generally to be found in the studio of those who cry—"Come buy my himages." Upon taking a turn towards the factory, he must needs call for his musket and his pagan reliques, which he slung over the left shoulder and marched up to me (to the melody of a lot of little bells attached to his gun), with the confidence of an honest man. I arose as well as I could, and expressed my gladness at having heard of his innocence. He had not stood before me many minutes before an old lady ran up and fondly embraced him; they both wept. It was his mother, and thus he felt, as—

> " bleakest rock upon the loneliest heath
> Feels, in its barrenness, some touch of spring;
> And in the April dew, or beam of May,
> Its moss and lichen freshen and revive;
> And thus the heart, most seared to human pleasure,
> Melts at the tear, joys in the smile, of woman."
>
> BEAUMONT.

Scarcely had the tears been banished, when the drum was thumped and his princeship marched forwards to Aboh, where he intends to make a sacrifice to his father and to his go-mhor. He bought a small cask of rum for the purpose of going the full hog whilst he can, for he well knows that Ajie is only anxious for his little capital.

I have a little fellow staying with me until some oil is paid, and who cannot be more than eight years of age, so fond and steadfast to his paganism that, having heard me give an order to have a sheep killed, he advanced, and blithely told me that he is not permitted to stay where a beast is killed. This is a good idea to propagate amongst the slaves, as it allows their masters an excuse in feeding them solely upon a yam a-day.

10th.—In England we have dumb-bells and other gymnastic exercises—not forgetting the noble art of self-defence—to develope our muscles and brace up our energies for the battle of life; but the Nigerians consider our manly practices unequal in effect to the following mode:—Preparatory to a young man entering upon his career, it is requisite that he should prove himself a man, and worthy of disdaining his mother's apron-strings. To prove this, he must undergo, in a state of nudity, a public bastinadoing. The bastinado is generally made of raw hide, plaited, and dried in the sun. The hero is then brought forward, and placed in the centre of the assemblage, with his hands placed upon his head; the thrasher then appears, and commences the flagellation to the extent of two dozen lashes; and should the young fellow endure the full amount without flinching, he is then applauded and escorted to his home, where a deputation of damsels await him, and offer themselves for his choice. But woe to the individual should he show signs of feebleness, for then he is disregarded and voted too young; but, be it as it may, the victim of this infatuation rarely escapes without a lacerated back, which necessarily confines him to his chamber for some time. I saw a young fellow to-day who had been fool enough to undergo the punishment (by which he won three wives, free of any other expense), and a pitiful sight he presented. I need not say otherwise than

> "None but the brave
> Deserve the fair."

11th.—The finale to Prince Arraboude's spree amongst the go-mhors and others has been of fatal moment to five parties. A gentleman having had reason to upbraid one of his mistresses for her want of decorum upon several occasions, and such censure being publicly applauded, she determined to do something to warrant approbation, and expiate her folly. She proceeded to the house of her liege lord, whom she found enjoying himself with his other wives and several associates. This was the right time for her to test his mettle, which she did by saying—"If you are a man, await my return." The husband did as requested, and presently she returned with a keg of gunpowder, which she placed in the centre. Having proceeded thus far, neither the husband nor wife dare retreat from their intention, which the lady shortly made manifest by applying a lighted torch to the keg, which instantly ignited, and blew five persons, the victims of wedlock included, into eternity.

12th.—The rainy season has fairly set in, and a very anxious time it is to me, on account of the diseases so rife here. Men and women are dying or dropping off very much like the leaves in autumn. The river occasionally presents a most disgusting sight upon its surface. If you look for a brief space of time, you will most probably see a number of human carcases floating down, the victims of illness and the butcher's knife. In the morning you may perchance meet with an individual to all appearance sane, but await his return towards evening, and ten to one you find in him the attributes of madness. This is no singular instance, but one of frequent occurrence.

Prince Tschukerma has kindly consented to assist me in erecting a good-sized salt-store for an equivalent of twenty pieces of cloth.

This evening I had the pleasure of witnessing the following signs of bereavement displayed by a comely widow whose husband had departed this life three days ago. Be it known that a lady assuming the weeds must, for three days after the event, retire and dwell in solitude upon the beach. At the end of the time she must uproot her abode, and cast it into the river. Her eyes are bound to follow the floating wreck until such time as she has been thoroughly drenched by her attendants (generally men) She is then escorted to the mansion of the deceased, and begins on the fourth day to give vent to her feelings (of happiness) in tears. This mockery of grief must also extend to three days, at the expiration of which time she retires from the busy world for the space of three months, during which all tributes of condolence must be duly rendered, for at that period she is in the market, and available to any aspirant to her hand and fortune. I am very sorry that I cannot offer myself. Having a pre-engagement in another country is perhaps a sufficient compensation.

13th.—Nothing of note to record save the many canoe-arrivals, laden with oil and other produce. I have also heard that the natives of Iddah are about to wage war against the Abohnites on account of their depredations.

14th. — Sunday, and a very miserable day. My assistant went to town, and met his satanic highness Ajie, who kindly asked after my health. He seems to feel the loss of my friendship, and wants to come to an understanding before the ship comes; but as I expect her arrival shortly, I deem it more prudent to defer all treaties until that period, when I trust they will make him return an ample repayment for his ill-gotten gains. His niggers are running away daily; so much so, that he is fearful of my possessing charms to aid their escaping, for he cannot recover them.

15th.—I caught a most curious fish to-day. When I drew it out of the water its stomach and chest expanded to a most unseemly size By so doing it resembled the well-known caricature of the man in the moon. It possesses very protruding lips, and four sharp incisors. Its eyes, of a greyish brown, seemed issuing from their sockets. Upon my immersing it in water, it immediately resumed its former shape and size. Its back is a mixture of green and yellow, and most peculiarly striped with black streaks. I believe the natives dry the belly coat for the purpose of making drumheads. The flesh of the largest is eaten, but they say that its gall is a most deadly poison. The Nigerian appellation given to it is occaejor, or the drummer-fish. The Abohnites believe that the inmates of the water have pastimes somewhat similar to their own, and as they possess a drummer to stimulate the dance, so do they bestow that dignity and title upon my finny treasure. I have heard this fish utter a sound resembling a buzz, buzz, but I do not profess to credit the theory maintained by my informants, that it is capable of speech. After remaining in the water for some hours, it breathed its last, and I stripped him of his coat and stuffed it.

16th.—This day opened with coolness, but as the day waned, it became very warm. In the shade it was about 80 degrees. During the night it rained very heavily.

17th.—Arose this morning, and met the rain pouring down in torrents; and a very miserable period of the year it seems to be. The natives are filthy and shivering, and in such a state of semi-starvation are they, that their very ribs are perceptible, and so polished at their extremities as to resemble Mister John Thomas's coat and buttons.

The gentleman mentioned by me on the 6th ultimo, aided by his jue-jue of medicals and cowries, has been successful in catching one of the thieves who had stolen his oil, but none of it could be recovered; and such being the case, he was necessitated by feelings of revenge to strip the fellow naked, bind him to a stake, and administer to his back two dozen lashes; lashes they may be, if unmercifully pommelling a man with sticks be a significant strappado. After so doing, they ornamented the person of the culprit with a chain of broken pots, and there left him to cool down. In the course of an hour he was as cool as a cucumber, and was then ducked in the river until rendered insensible. His eyes were then filled with pepper, and he was allowed to depart, not in peace, but under a shower of broken pots and swish.

Many of my readers will not be surprised to learn that the generality of Africans are very tasty hairdressers, trimming up the heads of their patrons with the admirable skill of a gardener. I never met a Nigerian but whose head was ornamented with small even and regular patches of wool. Chancing acutely to watch a professor of this charming art, acting with his tools upon a young scion of a noble house, I became interested, and discovered to my dismay that those parts only free from wool, were free from lice; therefore, as further experience has shown to me, whenever you see a native with a well-thatched skull, approach him not, unless you are anxious to increase your store of live stock.

May 31st.—Nothing worthy of notification having occurred up to this date, my Journal must necessarily fall short of its complement of news; but last night, and a few nights ago, a desperate attempt was made by several Abohnites to break into my store, but very fortunately they aroused me, and I had the good fortune to capture one of them, a stout, lusty Abcangar-marked fellow. Knowing that resistance would be in vain, and his confederates having made good their escape, he kindly consented to be handcuffed, and I honoured him with a seat upon my hencoop, where he now is, with a stout weight attached to his wrists. The other fellows I also know, but one is quite enough to feed. My canoe was also stolen from the wharf, and owing to the darkness of the night I have been unable to trace it out, but I have several scouts on the look-out, and woe betide the thief should he be found. The cry of Richard—

> "My horse, my horse, my kingdom for a horse,"

shall not equal the blubbering the strength of my strappado shall produce.

The river has also begun its rise, and I begin to look anxiously for the ship's arrival. May she ascend in safety, for I believe the natives of Orue are determined to kill all they can; in fact, they have on several occasions visited my factory, to my chagrin, but that soothing persuader, my revolver, generally makes them run. The weather is very rainy, and extremely unhealthy.

Provisions are also very scarce; my daily meals consisting, at this present time, of mashed yam and a red herring. I would advise any settler out here to provide himself with a cask or two of salt pork and beef, as with that, in conjunction with a yam, a man may subsist most heartily, and above all, he would be enabled to soar above obligation to a native. If you are in want, you must either starve or suffer imposition to the full realization of the term.

June 3rd.—By some friendly aid or other, the prisoner managed to escape this morning, handcuffed to a 56lb. weight.

Master Ajie has sent to inform me that he has found my canoe (query, did not his slaves steal it?) and that he wished to know what I intended to do about it. My reply was, take my thanks to your master, and tell him that my canoe is in good hands, and should he bring me the thief or thieves, then I will talk about his remuneration. It seems very strange to me that Ajie should have known my canoe, he never having seen it; but from what my friend Tschukerma says, the canoe was stolen, that Ajie might have some pretext for a conversation with me, and so damp my efforts to inform the agent of his rascality.

June 5th.—For the last two or three days I have been confined to my bed with a most alarming swelled face and head, the cause of which I cannot otherwise define than the unhealthfulness of the period.

My good old friend Tschukerma called upon me privately, and informed me that he had taken upon himself to restore me my canoe, and also to learn the cause of its being stolen. He said the parties who stole it had been authorized by Ajie so to do, in hopes of obtaining an extortionate demand: but failing in this, they see no other chance of quarrelling than by detaining the canoe under the plea of their having "dashed" the late Mr. Fairweather two bullocks, and he not returning the compliment, they deem it prudent to hold my canoe until an equivalent is paid. Another plea is, that Mr. Lyall obtained an accordion from the late Azakah, and the said accordion having been paid to John Locke on account of woman palaver by Mr Lyall, they deem it prudent to detain the canoe until an equivalent is paid. The third plea is, that a boy from Anjiamie, named Eifie, having left the factory and having joined the retinue of Hootie and the ship having taken a substitute in the person of an Abohnite, they deem it prudent to detain the canoe until an equivalent is paid. All this is known, and secretly urged by Ajie, who sees no other way of quarrelling than by means of these inventions. So far let him persevere, and I'll be bound to say he will die at last.

6th.—Nothing new.

7th.—Ditto, ditto.

8th.—Men engaged building and repairing the premises and outhouses. Very windy, cool, and rainy.

June 9th.—Whilst standing with Tschukerma, who was acting as overseer of the labourers, my attention was drawn by a loud murmur of voices and a coming crowd of Abohnites. Scarce had I turned round, than before me stood the prisoner who had so lately by some aid escaped from me. He was gagged and tied in a most inhuman manner; his body was covered with lacerations, and the blood was flowing copiously. His eyes were inflamed, and, in fine, he presented the most picturesque model of Nigerian brutality that I ever wish to see. Advancing with his princeship, we inquired the cause, and, after the man was unbound at our request, we learnt that the prisoner had made away with some twelve bags of salt belonging to his master, and that master being rendered fiendish thereby, had given a peremptory order for the man to die. His death was to be assured by drowning him in the Niger, and had it not been for the aforesaid intercession, this would most assuredly have been his fate. Suffice it to say that Tschukerma became the bondsman until the thief could procure double the amount of the salt stolen as a requital for the theft.

Rumour with her hundred tongues has been industriously circulating a report that two men belonging to our ship, the *Rainbow*, had been killed by the denizens of Orue.

This act seems to provoke and to stimulate many little acts of bravado, and under which I have to suffer many little traits of brutality. It is very pleasant for a lonely European resident, in a pagan land and surrounded by a band of atheistical brutes (to whose whims and caprices the said European is beholden for succour and the life he maintains), who, like vaulting ambition, overleap themselves, and tumble upon the lonely one with a depressing weight of violence and wrong; it is pleasant for a man, and an Englishman too, to hear his countrymen branded with the name of cowards, and by a set of nonentities whose whole stock in trade consists of theft and a matchet. Master Akie, above all, with his train of one hundred niggers, wives, and the piccaninnies to boot, declared boldly and flatly that we were afraid to resent the murders aforesaid, and those of the Messrs. Car, Parkes, and Lander. The many others who have fallen a prey to the pestilential clime of Africa are of course not to be mentioned. "What," said Akia, "you build ships and call yourselves white men and freeborn, and yet ye are afraid to resent the injuries you have received. In course of time we shall have you all killed, and your ships will remain as islands in the river. Ah, ah! you talk of what will be done; but talking will not build a town."

"No," said I; "but it may cause one to be broken."

Thus we ended a sweet half hour, devoted to nothing else than braggadocia. The people in Aboh are so infatuated with the success that crowns the natives of Orue, that they begin to feel a hankering for some such hostility. It is no wonder that such men should form such ideas of their own abilities when they find that the crimes of murder, theft, and other etceteras, to say nothing of indignities suffered upon any available occasion, are rewarded by the receipt of a bullock, a promise of redress, and a smiling request for plenty of oil. There have been six lives sacrificed in the river, and several brutally ill-used, and yet Britannia rules the deep and leaves such affairs unsettled. What is the use of spending an immensity of money in the attempt to suppress the slave trade, when the most interested know that such doings are fruitless? The money that has been expended in such pursuits might have paid part of an old score (the national debt). Asylums might have been raised, schools endowed, and the children of poverty in a better ordered state. The money really consumed in such fruitless endeavours would very soon amount to the sum total for the purificaction of old Father Thames, who occasionally rises from somnolence and tweaks us by the nose. The same sum would pave our highways, light our byways, and do (or cause to be done) many of those little necessities that creative though unfortunate genius may demand. Look at Ireland! Had a quarter of the sum spent in the aforesaid fruitless endeavours been used in the recovery of that nationality, Ireland would have raised her head, her children would arise, and fresh laurels would have encircled the brow of Old England We do not buy slaves; but why should we try to prevent others by blockading such commerce? It not only enhances the price of slavery, but it makes their sales romantic pleasure. The natives of Africa know that we are free-and-easy going coaches, and as such they intend to convert our "presumptions" into vehicles of ridicule. Open your eyes, will you, Mr. Bull, for the time is coming when your youngsters will sagely ask, where has all the money gone? A bauble is the fruit, and that bauble a costly one for years, is entitled, Slavery suppressed by the most incomprehensible means known.

My assistant has been in town all day hunting after affacas, a species of native matting for house roofing, but it was so scarce that he had to mount horse and so turn them up.

Weather cool, evening balmy, and greets the olfactories with Abohnian sweetness.

"Oh, thine incomparable."

11th.—I have now been out twelve months, and I must say that I long for my home, and a glance at those few familiar faces that once were fair to view. After my solitary residence, it is no wonder that the African trader, whose nostrils are now satiated with palm-oil, wishes once more to snuff the perfumes and the gales of his native clime. The past twelve months have formed an era in my existence never to be forgotten. I now live to thank my God for his providence in guiding me through my many dangers, for none who have patiently read my Journal can feel that my Nigerian life has been aught else but one of manifold danger and difficulties, as I have shown. I have been in imminent danger of my life, but always, by a supreme and providential interference, I have evaded such destruction. The scenes I have witnessed, the murders I have seen, in my solitary existence amongst this generation of pagans, bid me long for better things, and cry, "God protect the right." In the course of a few days I shall write finale to this my first volume, trusting that it has repaid the reader for his or her perusal by giving them an idea in its mildest form of what an African trader must act to procure that almighty want, a living Ah!

> "Ye gentlemen of England,
> Who sit at home at ease,
> Little do ye know
> The dangers of the seas."

The following brief description may serve to realize the appearance of an African damsel of the present century. Towards two o'clock about half-a-dozen damsels, the boast of Aboh, called to salute me, the first and foremost being Miss Ohginnie, a yellow-skinned, bright-eyed girl of some eighteen years. The next was Miss Amminnah, a lady of the blackest hue, and who wore her wool in the most *recherché* style, dressed by the Abohnian tonsor. It had reached the unparalleled length of two feet. A small wicker frame, built like a sugar-loaf, was perched upon her head, and the wool plaited and woven so as to cover the basket completely. The extremities had been worked into a tidy pigtail, and highly greased, as was her body. She was not the sweetest scented damsel one would wish to meet with, but she was so affable and rife with native airs and graces, that you were content to smoke a pipe and treat her civilly. These damsels, besides possessing a highly polished skin, wore immense circlets of ivory, and a pyramidal cone of brass rods upon either leg. Their wrists boasted not of bracelets otherwise than a huge hoop of ivory, of some two pounds weight each. Their arms also bore a cone of brass rods, and very picturesque they really looked. These ladies (as most African females do) chewed snuff in no inconsiderable quantities, in fact their teeth were so discoloured as to render them very unsightly. I was repeatedly invited to take a pinch, which I obliged them by doing, but placing it to my nose, and sneezing, the ladies laughed outright. I had also an opportunity of watching the native mode of snuff-manufacturing, performed by one of their attendants, who had brought their utensils and begged the tobacco from me. Setting herself down, and cleaning a highly-polished flat stone, she placed thereupon the stalks of three leaves. These she pounded and rubbed with a circular stone until a fine powder was the result, to which she added a small walnut-sized piece of potash, and pounded it also. She then proceeded to fill her bottle; but it being a disgrace to any female who cannot fill her snuff-box, she was obliged to re-commence her titillating powder-making until her hive was supplied. After a stay of some three hours the ladies arose, and I escorted them some half-a-mile. Upon leaving them I made a slight inclination, and raised my turban (ye gods! where are my hats?) and, strange to say, my salute was returned by a native curtsey.

Monday, the 12th day of June, must now close this present part of my Journal, but I do so in hopes, that should I stay out here for another year, to be able to give my readers an improved notion of my neighbours. In conclusion, I have but to say that there is a wide field open for the successful issue of trading, and, with a little skilful management on the part of the home authorities in providing their agents with suitable energetic and trustworthy assistants. We want no fellows who, when in feather, presume above their business; but we want men that will work as well as eat. Let a nod be as good as a wink to them. Let us have protection, and provisions, and plenty of hands to complete our task, and there will not be much to complain of. The present notion of trade is one of irregularity and privation, and if under such unfavourable auspices the trade pays, why should it not become more profitable by the addition of perseverance? Our present system is unorganized, and susceptible of great and pleasurable improvement. For instance, I have surmounted the most glaring difficulties; as by reference to this volume it will be seen that I was left totally unprovided for; without food, arms, or assistance, further than that of two coloured boys (I cannot call them men); had no interpreter, and I was bound to shift for myself. Had my presence of mind deserted me, perhaps I should now be added to the defunct, and my bones made into jue-jues; and as to the numerous robberies, and the brutality I have suffered, I cannot blame the natives—they are prone to evil —but rather the blame should attach itself nearer home, for I cannot believe that any man conscientiously would leave his property in such a neglected and forlorn condition as I found here. The natives are fond of trade, but they like plenty of it, not as we are circumstanced at present. During the stay of the ship we are as busy as Beck's wife, but when she has gone with her cargo, the refuse of stock left behind is either unsaleable, or too high a figure to be disposed of. I like small profits and quick returns; they pay the best; but that is not thought of. Oil is what we want, and as we carry on trade at this present we shall not have it. I pity the poor unfortunate devil who may be so situated. Alexander Selkirk was monarch of all he surveyed, but here the case is changed. Oeboe becomes the dupe of all who survey him, and through what? Why, the want of reform. It is absurd to leave a man in a state of abject poverty, and expect him to build a castle. But let me not digress too far.

It is sufficient to know that without food men cannot work, and without men work cannot be done.

Having said so much, I now take leave of my courteous readers. Perhaps we may meet again.

THE END.

For EU product safety concerns, contact us at Calle de José Abascal, 56–1°,
28003 Madrid, Spain or eugpsr@cambridge.org.

www.ingramcontent.com/pod-product-compliance
Ingram Content Group UK Ltd.
Pitfield, Milton Keynes, MK11 3LW, UK
UKHW012347130625
459647UK00009B/595